Contents

All Things
Bright and Beautiful?

All Things Bright and Beautiful?

A sociological study of infants' classrooms

RONALD KING
Reader in Education
University of Exeter

JOHN WILEY & SONS
Chichester · New York · Brisbane · Toronto

Library of Congress Cataloging in Publication Data:

King, Ronald, 1934–
  All things bright and beautiful?

  Bibliography: p.
  Includes index.
  1. Interaction analysis in education. 2. Education, Primary—Social aspects—Great Britain—Case
studies. 3. Teacher–student relationships.
4. Educational sociology—Great Britain. I. Title.
LB1731.K54   370.19′3   78-4518

ISBN 0 471 99653 X (cloth)
ISBN 0 471 99654 8 (paper)

Photosetting by Thomson Press (India) Limited, New Delhi and
printed and bound in Great Britain by The Pitman Press Ltd., Bath.

To my children,
Sarah, Martin, and Laura,
from whom I learnt so much

Acknowledgements

My main thanks go to the teachers in the three schools who generously allowed me to observe in their classrooms, and to the headmistresses who willingly gave me help and cooperation. They not only made possible the research upon which this book is based, but also made it a pleasant and rewarding experience. I have respected their confidences by the customary use of pseudonyms.

I also thank my daughter Sarah for her help which gave her an introduction to social research, David Hartley for his permission to quote the recorded interview in Chapter 13, and my secretary Karen Brewer who prepared the typescript and transcribed the tape-recordings with the skill of a code-breaker.

Contents

Introduction

The room has a single door bearing the label 'door'. The walls are almost completely covered with paintings of houses, trees, people, dragons, a list of the days of the week, and a collage labelled 'Humpty Dumpty'. Humpty Dumpty is composed mainly of broken eggshells stuck into an oval shape. The King's Men are of crêpe paper and milk-bottle tops, and the wall is of painted egg boxes. Models of fish are suspended from the light fittings. On various flat surfaces are displayed collections of cones, seeds, shells, and other natural objects.

The room contains 30 children of both sexes aged between five and six. Some are painting at easels, others make constructions from large wooden bricks, do jigsaw puzzles, carry out operations with pieces of coloured plastic, pour dry sand from one container to another, or write with pencils in books labelled 'busy books'. Some sit on chairs, others on the floor, which is partly carpeted, some walk from place to place. Some are silent, some talk to themselves or to other children.

A woman is seated on a small chair surrounded by a group of children. She holds up a card with 'house' written in large letters. About half the children put up their hands. She says, 'Gary.' A boy says, 'Horse.' She says, 'Is it?' He says, 'House.' 'Very good,' says the woman and hands him the card. 'How many have you got now?' He counts, 'One, two, three, four, five.' 'Five, that's lovely!' During this activity she glances around the room from time to time. Some children meet her gaze. She says in a voice that all can hear, 'I think someone is being silly.' A girl who has been flicking water from her wet hands looks at her and then dries them on a paper towel. The other children look at the woman and then at the girl.

Sitting in the corner of the room on a small chair is a man. He looks around the room and from time to time writes in a notebook. The children and woman neither talk to nor look at him.

The room is a classroom in an infants' school. The children are pupils, although the woman, their teacher, never refers to them as pupils but as children, 'my children'. The man is me. This is a descriptive fragment of the situation of the research which forms the basis of this book.

The events that lead up to my doing the research were briefly as follows. In 1970 I received a two-year grant from the Social Science Research Council for a study of forms of post-16 education. (Reported in the book, *School and College*, published in 1976.) Research only proceeds if people agree to be researched, and so when a college principal belatedly refused to help us I found we had a little spare research capacity. We had a research interest in the tertiary college that was being set up in the former local authority at Newbridge. The creation of this college, for all post-16 education, was accompanied by the reorganization of the secondary schools for the 12–16 age range, the junior schools from the 7–11 to 8–12 age range, and the infants' schools from the 5–7 to the 5–8 range. We had already surveyed the secondary schools and so it seemed a good idea, although frankly a speculative one, to use the unexpected research capacity to look at the primary schools before they were reorganized, with some vague plan, new research funds permitting, to return to them after the changes.

After some periods of observation in primary schools outside the area, we—that is, my assistants, Joan Fry and Bonnie Lucas, and I—made our survey in Newbridge in the summer of 1972. The headteacher completed a questionnaire about the school and was later interviewed. Every teacher in the school was interviewed about his or her work, using a loosely structured schedule. The head of one junior school would not help us (a response that came as no surprise to other heads who heard about it) and two others (also heads of junior schools) refused us permission to interview their teachers. The results of this survey, relating to all 18 infants' schools or departments, are referred to in the book, but, it must be stressed, from a relatively unimportant part of the material used.

The preparations for the survey stimulated my interest in what was going on in the primary schools, and so I applied to the S.S.R.C. for a grant for two years to extend the work to other areas using the Newbridge survey as a pilot. My application was rejected on the grounds that I was not asking for enough time or money to fulfil my plan. However, I was not disappointed because by that time my experience of going into the schools had made me see that what was required was not an extension of the survey but a more detailed approach to a smaller number of schools.

Two other factors helped me make this decision. First, I was becoming dissatisfied with the kind of research I had been doing for some years, which involved research assistants, large-scale surveys, and computerized data. I was feeling rather estranged from the research process, somewhat out of control. I wanted the refreshment of doing something on my own, in my own way, in my own time. The second factor was the changes occurring in the sociology of education.

Sociologists of education have a dilemma when they write books. Who are they writing for: a readership of sociologists or a non-specialist one of teachers and students? There is the necessity to present theories, methods, and results for academic approval, and the desire to reach as many readers as possible. I am not sure that the dilemma can be solved and both kinds of reader satisfied. However, I have attempted to orientate this book more towards the non-sociological reader, with the particular exception of Chapter 14 which compares my work with that of others concerning the sociology of infant education. The discussion that follows of the changes in the sociology of education that have a bearing on my research is therefore only a brief outline.

In the early 1970s criticisms began to be made that sociologists of education had neglected the study of educational knowledge and the classroom. This so-called 'orthodox' sociology of education had used large-scale surveys and quantified data rather than interviews and observations. Its critics, including Dave Gorbutt (1972), representing the 'new' sociology of education, made the accusation, not altogether correctly, that its basic theory was that of structural-functionalism. Functionalist theories explain social activities in terms of their contributions to the cohesion and maintenance of society. Since most children leave the educational system to enter jobs, education is explained, for example by Talcott Parsons (1961), in terms of its functions of selection and allocation, in relation to the occupational system to which it is 'adapted'. This input–output analysis meant that the processes of teaching and learning were neglected.

The 'new' sociology was mainly based upon social phenomenology. The social phenomenology particularly associated with Alfred Schutz (1932, 1972) emphasizes the interpretation of the assumptions and rules which make everyday life possible, and eschews explanations of social situations which involve external elements. In contrast to functionalism which emphasizes society as an external constraint on its members, social phenomenology stresses the way those members create society by their actions.

Many studies, including those of classrooms, have now been made using phenomenology, and its near relatives symbolic interactionism and ethnomethodology. Overall, these small-scale studies present a fragmented picture of society, which, in emphasizing the importance of the here and now, have tended to neglect events in the past and external social constraints. This kind of criticism, made, for example, by Geoff Whitty (1974), has been particularly associated with a proposed 'corrective'—marxist theory. Thus in addition to the 'orthodox' and the 'new' we now have a 'radical' sociology of education.

My colleague Stephen Mennell (1974) has written, 'To say anything about Marx is to step into a minefield of ideological controversy, and any brief statement is bound to be disputed by some.' A very brief and cautiously made statement about marxist theory would be that it proposes that the economic infrastructure of ownership and the means of production largely determines the social and cultural superstructure, including education. Thus, in the words of Marx, education in a capitalist society is a 'tool of ruling class interests'.

Burton Clark (1962) somewhat cynically observed, 'Never run after a bus, a woman, or an educational theory—another will be along soon.' Whatever its truth with respect to the first two it is clear that education buzzes with ephemeral fads and fashions. Non-sociologists may, with some justification, say the same for sociology. Some of the confusion they may feel is shared by students of sociology who want to understand these various theoretical positions without first taking sides.

My own response has been to further develop a theoretical approach based upon the sociology of Max Weber. In my previous research (1973, 1976a) I drew upon his concepts of power, authority, bureaucracy, ideology, social action, class, status, and party, and some of these are used in this study. I also use some elements of Schutz's work, who took Weber's social action as one of his starting-points. It is not my intention to explain or justify my approach at this stage. Instead I prefer to introduce the concepts in conjunction with the report of the researches with which they are bound. This is not the place to attempt to the justify a Weberian approach to education—an excellent start has already been made by Randall Collins (1977)—although I hope that this book will help the cause.

I have outlined the events leading up to the research; I will now outline how it was done. In September 1972 I asked the headmistress of a large infants' school with 14 teachers in Newbridge if she would allow me to make observations in one of the classrooms. I was not able to give her any clear idea of what I was trying to do, because I did not know exactly myself. I was intrinsically interested in a part of education which at that time was virtually unresearched. My preconceptions were based on the survey carried out the previous summer, the results of which had not been processed, my children's reported experience of their infants' school (all trained participant observers), and my own faded experience of being an infant pupil in an earlier historical period.

Mrs Brown, the headmistress of the Burnley Road school, introduced me to my first teacher, Mrs Pink, who generously let me into her classroom. After a first brief visit, I returned for longer periods leading to whole days. Over the first few weeks I learnt how to observe, and also began to formulate what the research was about.

I rapidly learnt that children in infants' classrooms define any adult as another teacher or teacher surrogate. To avoid being engaged in conversation, being asked to spell words or admire pictures, I evolved the following technique. To begin with I kept standing so that physical height created social distance. (I noticed how the teacher often got down to their level.) Next, I did not show immediate interest in what the children were doing, or talk to them. When I was talked to I smiled politely and if necessary I referred the child asking a question to the teacher. Most importantly, I avoided eye contact; if you do not look you will not be seen.

These measures were taken for two reasons. First, to enable me to observe uninterrupted and to make notes of my observations. My practice was to make my first visit to a classroom a short one in which I made no notes. This was to allow the teacher and the children respectively to get over any unease or curiosity. I soon found it possible to note incidents almost as they occurred and take down significant exchanges of speech, although, since it is impossible to observe and note everything, an element of selection was involved. There are observation techniques which may appear to be more scientific than the method I used. These are particularly associated with the interaction analysis of Ned Flanders (1970), where the observer sits recording at precise time intervals tiny items of individual behaviour, every smile, nod, frown or expression of disapproval. This kind of method only permits the seeing and hearing of things which have been decided in advance, and makes it difficult to grasp the flow of action. Although they are quantifiable they do not necessarily explain what has been observed.

Altogether I filled 32 notebooks with about half a million words of notes made during nearly six hundred hours with 38 teachers. Each evening I would make notes on the day's notes. Extracts from these notebooks form the core of the research reported here. These were made after an analysis of the notes (and other material) over a period of a year, and the reader must trust that I have made a fair and representative selection.

There are alternatives to note-taking in recording observations, including tape- and video-recording, film, and closed-circuit television. Financial resources and technical ignorance prevented my using the more sophisticated of these methods, but at their most useful they are only supplements to and not substitutes for direct observation and recording. In addition, they are artifacts in the situation which may distort it in unknowable ways. However, I did make some tape-recordings. These were with the knowledge of the teachers but not the children, recorders being easily concealed. The recordings were of teachers talking with the whole class or a group of children.

The second reason for my use of this non-participant observation was to reduce the effect I may have had upon the events I was trying to observe. With experience I felt that I usually succeeded in effectively disappearing. The teachers would often remark to this effect. Other teachers coming into the classroom would not see me, as with time I was able to sit down, sometimes concealed behind, or even in the Wendy house. I asked the teacher if she felt my presence had altered things in any way; by the second visit the answer was usually no, although it was clear that she was sometimes a little self-conscious and perhaps even putting on a special performance, but this was rare.

I originally intended to observe in Mrs Pink's class over the school year to study developing relationships. However, it was clear by half-term that Mrs Pink was pregnant and so I changed my plan so that I observed all the classes, spending at least two whole days in each, which took me until the summer of 1973, during which time I moved from being an outsider to being an insider, or, as the headmistress put it, 'one of the family'. The observations became easier as my technique improved and as each successive teacher knew better what to expect. In addition to the classroom observations I spent time in the staff-room, playground, and attending events like the Carol Service and Open Day. There are situations where politeness forbids the taking of notes, and like William F. Whyte, in that classic of observation studies *Corner Boys*, I was obliged to invent new uses for the lavatory. No research is free from ethical problems, but in this case the teachers were well aware of my note-taking, and sometimes made jokes about it, pointing to the notebook in my pocket.

After the year at Burnley Road I repeated the process in a second school, Seaton Park, which had a different kind of catchment area. I decided to do this because I wanted to know which of my observations at Burnley Road were special to that school. For reasons which will be made clearer later (Chapter 13), I decided to move to a third school, Langley, serving a third kind of social area, beginning in July 1974 and finishing a year later. Social class differences in education were a major theme in the 'orthodox' sociology of education, and indeed have continued to be for both the 'new' and the 'radical' variants. The differences between the schools relate to this sociological concern, as well as to educational policies and issues, including compensatory education and Educational Priority Areas. Most of the book (Chapters 1 to 8) draws upon observations made in the three schools, and represents what they had in common. The differences between them are dealt with in Chapters 9 to 13 and some comparisons are made in Chapters 14 and 15, together with their sociological and educational significance.

I have already described how when I presented myself to Mrs Brown at Burnley Road I did not have a precise idea of what the research was about. All that I had in mind was a vaguely anthropological model of trying to understand life in the classrooms and the school. The key word in that sentence is 'understand'. It is not sufficient to document what goes on, who is involved, how and where it happens, but an attempt must be made to explain why. To answer the question 'why' involves some kind of theory. The sociological theory I used was action theory, of a fairly simple kind. This stems from the work of Max Weber (1964) who defined social action as 'all human behaviour when and insofar as the acting individual attaches subjective meaning to it'. For Weber the task of the sociologist is to understand the subjective meanings that people assign to their actions. The study of meanings (*Verstehen*) does not completely explain social life, not the least because actions have unintended and sometimes unrecognized consequences, but no explanation is acceptable without some reference to those meanings.

How is it possible to understand what another person means in doing something? Interpretations made purely on the basis of observations can be wrong; a man who makes a series of body movements by his bedside may be doing physical exercises or praying. The easiest way is to ask. Over a period of time with a given teacher I could see certain actions repeated. At breaktime, or more often after school had finished, I would refer to particular events, ask the teacher why she had acted in that way. My questions were never framed in the abstract ('What are your aims in teaching the children?'), sometimes as generalizations ('How do you know who is ready to read?'), but mainly related to specific events ('Why did you smack Freddie?').

This method was not without its problems for both me and the teacher. These were of two kinds. First, the relationship between the sociologist and the subject had to be learnt. Most adults who enter classrooms make value-judgements of what they see. The teacher may not know what these are but she knows they are being made. In addition, most of these adults are her status superiors, the headmistress, inspectors, advisers. By my demeanour and talk I tried to make it clear that my interest was in seeing what happened and in trying to understand why it happened, that I was not an expert in infant education, and that anything I saw or she said was confidential. Some teachers found it hard to understand why a grown man should choose to spend his time in the way I did, but after a few weeks in each school I was considered by most to be fairly benign and certainly no threat. The basis of the research relationship was that the teacher and I were the only adults to have witnessed particular events in her classroom. The relationship was based on a unique shared experience, and many teachers said they found it rewarding and useful to them.

The second problem in understanding the teachers' meanings arises from the nature of meanings. In the flow of social action and interaction we do not always reflect upon the meaning of what we are doing because we are too busy in the doing. Many meanings are held half-consciously and are sometimes difficult to make articulate. For the teachers their repeated day-to-day actions in the classroom were part of what they took for granted in the situation, a part of what every infants' teacher knows. Some questions about meanings were seen as questions about the obvious—the obvious to the teacher. Others may even have been seen as faintly absurd.

There are a great many actions to be observed and understood even in a short period of time in a classroom. My efforts were concentrated on those which occurred most frequently and which most teachers engaged in. The more I observed the more familiar and predictable things became. So although individual teachers were observed at work, the attempt was to understand infants' teachers as an occupational class of persons. When a reference is made to 'teachers', these are typical teachers. The kind of analysis does not deny that individual teachers varied in what they did and why they did it, and some indication of these variations can be made, but they are sometimes difficult to explain. There were those who in the opinions of their colleagues, and by my observations, were deviant teachers, and others who by the same criteria were better teachers than others (Chapters 6 and 8). There were also differences between the three schools (Chapters 10–13). However, the similarities between teachers were more obvious and arguably more important than the differences. These common characteristics, both within and between the three schools, were social in origin, and were therefore susceptible to sociological explanation.

At the end of each period of time in the three schools I discussed my work with the teachers as a group. This was an extension of the talk with each one individually. I presented to them the kind of analysis that is made in the rest of the book, with particular reference to the situation in that school. I invited them as a group to confirm my interpretation of the meanings they assigned to their actions, and for the most part they did so, although my formulations were sometimes rather strange to them.

There was a second purpose in these meetings. At the beginning of the research period I was trying to following some of the ideas of the American sociologists Glaser and Strauss from their book, *The Discovery of Grounded Theory*. Briefly, they propose that sociological theories should be 'grounded' on data generated by the act of research. Theory should not precede research but follow from it. I now have doubts about the feasibility of such a process (see Chapter 14), and would not necessarily claim to have used it successfully in this research. In addition, they propose that the theory so generated should make sense to those to whom the theory applies. Once again, I am not sure how this can always be done, but in this case it was a fairly satisfactory way of verifying my theories.

In addition, I have always been aware that the subjects of research give much to the researcher: their time, their opinions—they open up areas of their lives for inspection. I felt, if only on the grounds of politeness, I should give something back. The opportunity to talk about themselves with what I hope was an interested and sympathetic person with no authority over them was welcomed by many teachers. The group meetings were a way in which I as a guest for a year in each school explained what I had been doing; they also allowed me to present my explanations of what I had seen them doing. These meetings were also useful to the teachers in that they realized just how much they had in common with one another, and that many of what they as individuals defined as problems were problems for others too.

Although observations and interviews were my most important methods I also used the analysis of documents. All educational enterprises involve a great amount of paper. I analysed samples of children's writing and pictures, their reading and mathematics texts, and, with the headmistresses' permission, the school records, of which it was possible to make some quantification. All of these data were in a sense 'found'. Some 'created' data from social surveys, including the Census, are used in Chapter 9, dealing with the catchment areas of the three schools. There is no best method in sociology, only suitable and feasible methods. Frank Bechhofer (1974) has argued that as many methods should be used as possible, so that if all or most yield similar results, the researcher may be assured that they have some combined validity. It pays to be eclectic.

Apart from the opening paragraphs of this introduction children have been little mentioned and the impression may have been given that the study was only of teachers. But teachers are teachers in their interactions with pupils. Children's actions have subjective meanings for them. In every classroom there could be 30 other meanings being assigned to a given course of action or interaction, in addition to the teacher's. The enormity of the task of interpreting pupils' meanings of classroom activities makes it a difficult one, but in addition there is another problem. How is it possible to understand the subjective meanings of very small children? Anyone who has tried, as I have, will know that interviewing a 5-year-old is a difficult task. If teachers are unused to reflecting on their own actions young children seem to be almost incapable of doing so. However, it was possible to observe children's behaviour in the classroom and to listen to their talk (and sometimes to talk with them), and to judge to what extent their behaviour and their talk were related to the actions of their teacher. It was also possible to infer something of a small child's subjectivity by his or her emotional response to a situation. I assumed that a 6-year-old who cried was probably upset and one who laughed was happy, assumptions not always justified in relation to adults.

The children are central to this study because they were central to their teachers' concerns. The activities of the classroom were for the most part arranged and allowed by the teacher, and were based upon her ideas about the nature of children in general and of the particular child. In this respect teachers were very powerful, a term they would not accept because they felt that what they permitted to happen was both natural and best. However, the children were not mere cyphers in the situation. They were capable, even at the age of 5, of challenging the teacher's control of the classroom (Chapter 6), and, as the comparisons of the three schools show, the meanings that teachers assigned to particular pupils' characteristics had observable and significant consequences for what happened in the classroom (Chapters 10, 11, 12, and 13).

The Plowden Committee who reported on primary education in 1967 found that 'we heard repeatedly that English infant schools are the admiration of the world'. 'All Things Bright and Beautiful' was one of the children's favourite songs. Its use in the title of this book poses a figurative question about infant education, to which I hope the following chapters will enable the reader to make a more informed answer.

CHAPTER ONE

Infants' Teachers' Ideologies

Inside an infants' school classroom there is a recognizable social world, clearly different from, for example, the social worlds of the pavement or the playground. It is also different in many ways from the classrooms in other types of school. One of my research tasks was to describe this world, and also to try to explain it. To begin with, the task of recording events to make such a description was paramount. The explanations were tentatively formulated during this work, but only explicitly so towards the end of the three-year period of observations. In writing this, I am virtually reversing this process in presenting the theory first and the data afterwards.

This account of the how and why of infants' classrooms is presented as an ideal type in that it represents those actions and interactions that were commonly found to happen in most of the classrooms observed in the three schools. As will be seen later (Chapter 8), those classrooms where typical actions did not occur were very important in making and justifying explanations made about those where they did occur.

Most of the things that happened in the classrooms were arranged to happen or were allowed to happen by the teacher. Every arranged or permitted action had a subjective meaning to the teacher (as did every non-arranged and non-permitted action). I have already described how I attempted to get at these meanings by talking to each teacher about events that she and I had seen occur, and also by means of a general discussion with all the teachers in each school. Although, to modify a once popular song, it can be said that 'every little action had a meaning of its own', it was clear from my observations that despite the diversity of events there was a pattern to them. One teacher on my first visit to her class turned to me after a few minutes and said, 'What you'll make of it I don't know, but there is a plan underneath it all.' I wanted to work out and explicate that plan.

Little by little I began to discern it, and having done so it became obvious, so obvious that when I outlined it to the teachers it was regarded as unremarkable. The infants' teachers' actions were related to the ideas they held about the nature of young children and the nature of the learning process. These ideas, or ideologies, were seldom explicitly expressed by the teachers because to them they had the status not of ideas but of the truth. What they believed about children and education was integral to what they defined as real in the classroom. Social reality, what is 'real', is not usually a problem for people in a familiar situation, but it is a sociological problem to explain it.

In Weberian terms these ideologies were institutionalized in the form of what Schutz (1953) called recipes, that is, agreed sets and ways of doing things. These recipe ideologies were for the most part unconsidered by the teachers because they were taken for granted, but there were situations in which these ideologies were made more explicit. This was when they had to be justified to those who did not necessarily take them for granted. The teachers were seldom in this kind of situation, but the headmistresses sometimes were. I shall draw upon two sources of the explicit expressions of the ideologies by the headmistresses: letters written to parents, and guidance notes written for teachers when the infants' schools were reorganized to become first schools. Two other sources will also be quoted: first, the expression of the ideologies by experts which were available to the teachers, including notes for teachers in the books used in the schools; secondly, the official expression of these ideologies in the Plowden Report, *Children and their Primary Schools* (1967). I cannot say that all the teachers had read the report or agreed with it, but all three headmistresses had copies prominently displayed in their rooms. Two of them spoke of it most enthusiastically, one calling it her Bible: 'And I agree with every word in it.'

The official ideology of the Plowden Raport is essentially one of child-centredness.

At the heart of the education process lies the child. No advance in policy, no acquisitions of new equipment have their desired effect unless they are in harmony with the nature of the child, unless they are fundamentally acceptable to him. (p. 7)

The child is seen as passing through a naturally ordered sequence of physical, physiological, psychological, and social development, although each child possesses a unique individuality. Young children are naturally curious, exploring and discovering things around them, learning best through their play when they are happy and busy, and free to choose to do what is of interest to them. Education is seen as creating conditions which acknowledge these properties, and allow the full development of individual potential. Bernstein and Davies (1969) have called this the horticultural model of education. It is possible to distinguish a number of important elements that comprise the infants' teachers' child-centred ideology. These are: developmentalism, individualism, play as learning, and childhood innocence.

It was obvious to every teacher that over a period of months the children in her class grew bigger. This physical development was important in her orientation towards them, but in addition other kinds of development, particularly intellectual and emotional, were assumed to be taking place which were of educational significance. As the official ideology puts it:

Knowledge of the manner in which children develop, therefore, is of prime importance in avoiding educationally harmful practices and in introducing new ones. (Plowden Report, volume I, p. 7)

The kind of 'expert' evidence used by the Report to support this idea is also shown in this extract from the headmistress's notes for teachers at the Seaton Park school.

Piaget has realized just how limited is the child's capacity to think in the abstract.

At the level of the infants' teacher's recipe ideology, developmentalism is shown in this kind of incident recorded in my observation notes. Small boy picks up a work card from a tray. Teacher: 'You're too young to do those sums.' 'Growing up' was a common theme for teachers to choose as a class project. At Seaton Park it formed the basis of an assembly given by one class, in which they compared what they could do when they were babies with what they could do now.

Closely related to the idea of sequential development is that of readiness, particularly in relation to reading (Chapter 3), and of naturalism.

The average child reaches his peak of natural spontaneous activity at the age of seven. (Notes for teachers, Langley school)

The idea of individualism applies to children and to the way they are educated.

Individual differences between children of the same age are so great that any class, however homogeneous it seems, must always be treated as a body of children needing individual attention. (Plowden Report, volume I, p. 25)

In her notes for teachers the headmistress of Seaton Park put it this way:

Adaptability is vital—if your approach doesn't suit a particular child then change it—the approach not the child.

Learning through play is officially endorsed in the Plowden Report (p. 193):

Adults who criticise teachers for allowing children to play are unaware that play is the principal means of learning in early childhood.

The recognition that this idea of play is not held universally is also shown in this extract from a letter sent to parents of new pupils by the headmistress of Seaton Park.

Most of what adults would regard as play, is, in reality, of the deepest significance in the child's intellectual development.

The ideology in action is shown in this extract from my observation notes:

Two 6-year-olds play fish subtraction. Each has the same duplicated outline of a fish with circular scales, each scale marked with a number from 0 to 5. They take turns to throw two dice. Each subtracts the smaller number from the larger and then crosses out the answer on one of the scales, checked by his partner. The first one to cross out all the scales is the winner. I ask one of them what they are doing. He says, 'Playing fish.'

Closely related to learning through play are the ideas of interest, happiness, and 'busyness'.

Probably the best results in the teaching of reading are obtained by the teacher who uses the interests and enthusiasms of the child. (Notes for teachers, Seaton Park)

There is the idea that children learn best when they are happy.

Teacher in an interval between two activities: 'Let me see a smile. A good big one.'
(Observation notes)

Interested, happy children learning naturally through play manifest busyness.
The epitome of busyness is expressed in the words of a song written by the deputy
head of Burnley Road school for her class of 7-year-olds to sing as part of their
presentation of the school assembly.

You've got to get busy
When you get up in the morning,
You've got to get busy
When you go to school and work,
You've got to get busy,
Close your mouth and stop that yawning,
So roll your sleeves up right away
Don't shirk!

You've got to get busy if you're
Feeling sad and gloomy,
You can get busy in your home
Or here at school,
It's fun to be busy, so I hope you'll listen to me
Let being busy be your golden rule!

I missed the actual performance but I was honoured with a special one replete
with happiness.

The idea of childhood innocence had a special status in the ideology of infants'
teachers. It is not the case that the teachers regarded the children as being
incapable of doing things that they, the teachers, defined as being naughty or
wrong, but that the children, particularly the 5- and 6-year-olds, could not be
blamed for these things, because they had not yet developed the capacity to
control themselves. Young children were considered to be in a natural amoral
state and not fully responsible for their actions.

A girl complains to the teacher, 'Gary keeps flicking paint on my picture.' Teacher: 'I'm
sure he didn't mean to do it.' (Observation notes)

The state of innocence was not only recognized in the teachers' interpretations
of children's behaviour but also in the way they protected children from harmful
and unpleasant aspects of the outside world, and in the preservation of the world
of childhood in the face of adult reality, as the following example shows:

At news time a 6-year-old boy tells of his tooth coming out, and how he put it under his
pillow and woke up in the morning to find a 5p piece and the tooth gone. The teacher
asks, 'Where did the tooth go and the 5p come from?' The boy says, 'The fairies.'
Another boy has his hand up and is bursting to tell the 'truth': 'No it's not . . .!' The
teacher shushes him until he stops. Talking about the incident later she said, 'It's not up
to me to destroy his innocence.'

The desire to protect children from unplesantness was shown in the teachers'
management of the knowledge of death. The teachers at Burnley Road were
particularly keen on keeping pets in the classroom. When guinea-pigs became old
they were taken away from school by the teachers, partly because they tended to

get snappy when handled, but also to prevent their deaths being witnessed by the children. A gerbil in a cage outside a classroom died just as afternoon school was finishing. One girl noticed its death throes and asked, 'What's wrong with it?' The teacher replied, 'Oh nothing to worry about, you can go home now.' Later she said to me, 'Thank goodness they didn't see it.' A similar sentiment was expressed by the headmistress when the crossing patrol man collapsed and died in the office just before school started. She did mention his death in a school assembly a few days later, but I was unable to observe the occasion.

These ideas of innocence are not explicitly expressed in the Plowden Report, possibly because the Committee considered they were so widely accepted as to be unremarkable. However, on the basis of evidence to be presented later I suggest that it is the ideology of innocence that particularly marks off the infants' teacher from the junior school teacher (Chapter 8).

There are a number of important points that should be made about this analysis of teachers' classroom activities in terms of their ideologies. It is not being suggested that teachers' actions are determined by these ideologies: the image of the teacher as a programmed automaton or cultural dope (Garfinkel, 1967). Ideologies are both practical and evaluative, guiding both what is done and what should be done. Most of the teachers most of the time were reasonably content with the situation in their classrooms. The 'what was done' and the 'what should have been done' were fairly close. As an occupational group they seemed very secure in their professional beliefs and practices, as was demonstrated in their general readiness to allow me to observe them at work. One of the purposes of the Plowden Report was to propagate child-centred progressive education. Whereas from studies such as Neville Bennett's (1975) it is clear that among junior school teachers there is still a significant adherence to 'traditional' methods, among these infants' teachers the child-centred approach was axiomatic. They considered their contribution to the children's education to be the most important: the foundation for what was to come. Some even regarded the move to the junior or middle school almost as the end of real education. As one teacher put it, 'We have done our best by these children. Let them [the middle school teachers] do their worst.' However, circumstances will be described later in which this security was shaken, the gap between what happened and what ought to happen was wide, and the teachers' ideologies were strained (Chapters 10 and 11).

It should also be stressed that these ideas about the nature of education and of children have not always existed, and are not held universally: they are human social creations or constructs. Phillippe Ariès (1962) has shown that as recently as a century and a half ago babies were not considered to be human or even to exist in a social sense; there was no necessity for their deaths to be reported. Childhood was not seen as special stage of development; children were considered to be miniature adults. Far from being treated as innocent, they were more commonly seen as basically sinful. Pinchbeck and Hewitt (1973) illustrate this by the record from 1780 of a 7-year-old girl hung at Norwich for stealing a petticoat. The Victorian stories for children collected by Leonard De Vries made frequent reference to death and maiming in 'real-life' contexts.

The social history of infant education in this country is marked by the names of ideologues such as Pestalozzi, Froebel, Montessori, the McMillan sisters, and Susan Isaacs. The institutionalization of their child-centred ideologies into English infant education to be given the status of the 'truth' has been systematically traced by Nanette Whitbread (1972), but this 'truth' is not universally accepted. Play as a form of learning was certainly not believed by several headmasters of primary schools interviewed in the general survey (all of whom were junior and not infant trained). In talking about his infants' department, one said, 'It's all play down there. It's mainly matter of getting them used to school. All the learning takes place in the juniors.' The headmistresses of Burnley Road, Seaton Park, and the Langley schools all confessed a certain strain in their relationships with the headmasters of the junior (later middle) schools their children transferred to, leading on one occasion to an altercation over the phone. These ladies felt that their own and their teachers' methods were misunderstood and unappreciated. (This point is returned to in Chapter 14.)

Ideologies are held by particular groups of people, and provide an over-arching concept of their social experience. To take an example which will be returned to in the next chapter: the ideology of nudism denies that seeing people of the opposite sex with no clothes on can be sexually exciting. This idea is quite clearly not shared by most people, whether they go to strip shows and look at pin-up magazines, or wish to have such things banned. What is 'real' for nudists is not so for others.

The reality of the classroom for the teacher was constructed through her ideology. An understanding of this ideology, at the level of a set of everyday recipes for doing things, will be used to explain the various activities that take place in infants' classrooms. Ideologies also help to integrate the groups' members' conceptions of themselves, that is, their social identities (see Chapter 8). The child-centred ideology of infants' teachers not only defined the child, but also the teacher.

CHAPTER TWO

The Definition of the Situation

Social reality is created by human beings. The classroom reality of infants' teachers was to a large extent their own creation. This proposition is hard to accept when what is real is regarded as being external to people, as something 'out there', but it can be better understood by taking an example where what is 'real' may be defined in different ways. Most people consider that seeing members of the opposite sex with no clothes can be sexually exciting. But a minority deny this connection between nakedness and sexual arousal. These are nudists or naturists. The ideology of nudism, the set of ideas used to justify going around with no clothes on, asserts that there is nothing shameful in exposing the naked body, and that this can lead to feelings of freedom and natural pleasure, and to bodily and spiritual well-being. Martin S. Weinberg (1965) made a study of nudist camps and found little evidence of sexual impropriety. He showed how this aspect of the ideology of nudism was made real by the actions of the nudists themselves.

Nudists act in such a way as to preserve sexual modesty. The motives of applicants for membership of the clubs are carefully scrutinized, possibly during a trial period. Membership is often confined to families and married couples. A number of norms are observed by members. They do not stare at one another; sex talk, dirty jokes, and small group activities are taboo. Alcohol is banned and there are rules about not taking photographs without permission, and suggestive poses are frowned upon. Bodily contact as in dancing is taboo. Each of these actions contributes to maintaining the nudists' reality of nakedness having nothing to do with sex. This perfectly illustrates the conception of the definition of the situation as used by W. I. Thomas (1928). 'If men define situations as real, they are real in their consequences.' The definition of sex-free nakedness is made real by the actions of those who make the definition.

For Weber (1964) the study of subjective meanings of an action required an understanding of the ends that are being pursued and how the acting individual perceives they may be achieved. The habitual actions of everyday life, 'recipes' in Schutz's (1972) terms, are repeated because their ends usually are achieved. The 'definition of the situation' may be regarded as a neat and useful formulation of this.

Thomas's theorem forms the basis of my analysis and understanding of infants' teachers in the classroom and the school situation. What the following sections attempt to show is that by defining as real their ideas about the nature of children as being innocent, as possessing individuality and passing through sequential stages of development, and also by defining real learning as being child-centred, the teachers pursued actions which tended to confirm these as realities, that is, they were real in their consequences.

Defining the classroom

To enter an infants' classroom as a stranger is often to experience an educational casbah. The total content is enormous. With the assistance of my elder daughter I made a 26-page inventory of the contents of one classroom for 5–6-year-olds in the Burnley Road school.

The furniture consisted of 28 small chairs, two dumpy chairs, a large armchair, three round tables, two half-hexagonal tables, a small display table, a double-sided easel, a double-sided bookshelf unit, two large fixed cupboards, a wall blackboard, fixed shelving on two walls, and five assorted carpets. These were arranged so that there were three groups of tables and chairs, a library corner containing most of the 257 books, and a Wendy house, or home corner. A few classrooms had a Wendy house that looked like a house with doors and windows, but most, like this one, were areas marked off by an arrangement of furniture and containing, typically, a toy cooker, dresser, utensils, dolls, dolls' pram and cot, and dressing-up clothes.

The walls and cupboard doors were almost totally covered in children's paintings and collages, including a six-foot man made of crêpe paper and wool, printed sets of number pictures, and a picture alphabet. The various flat surfaces were covered in displays and collections of objects including shells, seeds, and birthday cards.

The open shelves contained many of the 22 jigsaws, boxes of animal cards, picture or picture–word lotto sets, coloured plastic or plain wooden geometrical, animal, tree, and house shapes, teacher-made picture story cards, sum cards, word cards, counting cards, tins of pencils, crayons, scrap paper, unifix, scissors, sticky paper, silver paper, and a set of scales. More of these things were stored in the two large cupboards and in 16 large wallpaper-covered cardboard boxes on a top shelf. Other contents included paint brushes, drinking straws, Christmas decorations, paper scraps, cotton wool, raffia, old newspapers, plastic bags, coloured card, pieces of material.

On the floor were large boxes of wooden bricks and crêpe paper. The junk box was full of assorted plastic and cardboard containers, such as cornflakes packets and yoghurt cartons. The sink was surrounded by paste pots and plastic containers, and underneath were stored a hand brush and plastic buckets. I will not exhaust the reader more by describing the rest of the contents of this one room, except to report that it included empty wine bottles, a candlewick bedspread, some polystyrene ceiling tiles, and a fairy for the top of a Christmas tree.

The physical set-up of the classrooms was not static. Teachers constantly changed the furniture around, created new displays, and recirculated material, games, and toys. The walls tended to be rather bare at the beginning of term but were often completely covered by the end, as this description from my notebook shows:

> The room is gorgeously decked for Christmas. The whole of one wall is a mural of angels (cut out from a template by the children), around a Nativity scene set up by the teacher, in which pupils' cut-outs of animals, trees, and houses form a part. Each child has made a cracker, a calendar, a Father Christmas, and a (paper) Christmas pudding. These are hung on the other walls and from the ceiling, together with paper chains cut by the children. (Girl informant)

The presentation of the classroom may be seen as the outcome of actions taken by the teacher. There were, however, some obvious constraints. The fixed physical amenities of the room—its size, windows, cupboards, sinks—were outside the control of the teacher. However, she could exercise some influence and choice, through the headmistress, in relation to movable furniture, books, games, stationery, and equipment. Most teachers in each of the three schools were satisfied with this provision, although many qualified this by saying they could always do with more. The few unsatisfied were those who were new to the school and to a particular room, and had not chosen its contents.

From the previous description it is clear that much of the content and its display was controlled by the teacher. Many brought in things from their own houses—old rugs, curtains to put over open shelving, magazines, toys and games their own children had grown out of. Children were encouraged to bring in useful things. The headmistress of the Seaton Park school sent a list of useful materials to parents asking them to send them in to the teachers. It contained 114 items, including icecream tubs, stockings, wallpaper, inner tubes, and old clocks.

Teachers created the physical set-up of their classrooms in accord with their recipe ideologies about the nature of children and their education. These were expressed by the headmistress of Seaton Park in her notes for teachers.

> Make your room an exciting and stimulating place to live . . . a specially devised environment which allows the children to be individuals, growing at a pace and in a way most suited to their individual capacities.

Children were defined as being naturally interested in things: in consequence the classroom was set up to evoke their interest. Children were defined as having individual propensities for learning: in consequence a wide range of educational material was provided.

Other aspects of the physical presentation of the classroom will be dealt with later, in particular its relation to the concepts that the teachers had about themselves as teachers. They used their classrooms to express their professional identities, and their classrooms were used by others to judge their performances as teachers (Chapter 8).

Classroom activities—defining work and play

The classroom was the physical setting for a profusion of activities. At first it was difficult to see the way these were structured. The timetable in each school controlled only the use of non-classrooms, such as the hall, television room, and maths workshop. The within-classroom activities were to some extent structured around these, and around the dinner and playtime breaks. Every day was phased into small divisions of time. Mrs Pink's day began with coming into class time, followed by hanging up coats time, then news time, register time, getting ready for first activity time. Getting ready for milk time preceded milk time, which lead to clearing away after milk time, and then going to the lavatory before playtime. The day included singing time, washing hands before dinner time, and ended with story time, putting on coats time, and finally good-bye time.

Activities were also structured in the way they were defined. These definitions represent a classification of educational knowledge. The headmistress of the Langley school listed twelve categories in her notes for teachers: reading, mathematics, number, science, nature, art, religious education, environmental studies, music, literature, writing, and physical education. Similar categories were used by the headmistress of the Seaton Park school. The teachers' operational definitions were similar but less distinct. There were two main reasons for this: the integrated day and the distinction between work and play.

Most teachers operated what they called an integrated day in which the various learning activities were intended to be 'integrated' into a whole so blurring them as distinct categories: a 'whole' curriculum to fit the 'whole' child. As in the survey reported by Peter Moran (1971) the idea was operationalized in many different ways, as the following dimensions indicate:

(1) The activities to be integrated differed in number and classifications; for example, writing, reading, number, and craft, or, writing, maths, reading, sounds, and choosing time.
(2) The pupils were sometimes grouped and the number of groups varied.
(3) The activities were followed in the same or different sequence by each group, or individual children, or sometimes the whole class.
(4) Individuals or, more rarely, groups could sometimes choose their own sequence of activities.
(5) The different activities could be precisely timed or had to be completed by a certain time, usually the end of the morning or day.

These many different arrangements, varying within as much as between the schools, were the outcome of the teachers' autonomy in the classroom, and allowed different degrees of autonomy to the children. The touchstone in every situation was to have as many different activities going on as possible. The ideal of every child doing something different is consonant with the idea of each child having a unique individuality which should be recognized in the learning process.

Amongst this diversity of ways of defining and organizing educational knowledge, the delineation of the basic skills of reading, writing, and number was always very clear. Whereas one teacher's craft was another's project work there was no doubt about the status of the three R's.

The second source of blurring of categories of learning was the distinction made between activities defined as play and those defined as work. The distinction was not a clear-cut one. In the group meetings with teachers there seemed to be no generally agreed definition, and this tended to lead to extended, inconclusive discussions. However, in observing teachers in action in the classroom it was possible to delineate their operational definitions. Each of these is illustrated by examples drawn from the many recorded.

Play as a prelude to work

This was applied to young children. Play was seen as helping them to settle in, and, in some cases, as a necessary developmental stage to be completed. 'He won't be ready to work until he has played for a bit longer.'

Play as a form of learning

Activities verbally defined as work by the teacher were also defined as such by the children, in that they too used the word for the same activities. However, when teachers defined play as learning this definition was not necessarily shared by the children. Some 5-year-olds were putting wet sand into small buckets and then turning out the casts. When asked they defined this as playing at sandcastles, but their teacher defined sandplay as building up concepts as a preparation for doing mathematics.

Play as a reward for working

'Vanessa, you can't play a game until you have finished your work card.'

Play may interfere with work, but not vice versa

'Wayne, people are working over there, so you must come over here to play.'

Play may be chosen, work cannot be refused

'Some of them would play all day, I have to get them to work'

Teachers define when work is completed

'That's not enough writing. Go away and write me another nice sentence.'

Work is done for the teacher

'Now I'd very much like some writing, please.' 'It's the first time I've had this [a sum card] done for me.'

Work is done in the mornings, play in the afternoons

In the survey of infants' teachers in Newbridge, 52 of the 100 interviewed reported they organized their day about the dinner hour. In the morning most of the 'work' was done. This was also called head work, the three R's, basics, academic things, and writing, number, and reading. The afternoon was the main time for 'play', or handwork, freer activities, games, messy things, projects or choosing time. Only one teacher reported doing 'work' consistently in the afternoons and not in the mornings.

Teachers work, they seldom play

Work activities were demonstrated by the teacher, for example writing or doing sums, or she practised them, as when reading. Teachers were potential models for work activities. My observations were that children often learnt to play from other children.

Play is more important for young children

This definition follows from those making play a prelude to work and form of socialization for school. It is real in its consequences in that classrooms for older children contained fewer toys and games than those for younger ones. 'They should be growing out of toys by now.' Wendy houses, home corners, and dressing-up clothes were not provided. The organization of time allowed for less play. Older children defined as needing to play less than younger ones were not allowed to play as much as younger ones, and so were never given the opportunity to demonstrate the same or even more 'need' for play. Teachers defined pupils' needs, and these definitions were real in their consequences.

This particular definition helps to explain the confusion among the teachers when they discussed play in the abstract. Most classes in these schools were mixed-age ones, sometimes called family or vertical grouping. Within the classroom the same activity could be defined as play or work, or defined as different kinds of play, according to the age of the child.

Playing in the classroom

Play was defined as a natural activity of children but the children were not allowed to define play for themselves. They were constrained by the toys and games provided, and by the teacher's active presentation of her definition of play.

Although the classrooms of younger children were equipped with many games and toys the teacher's selection of these indicated her view of play. Some were quite clearly didactic, for example, picture and word lotto. Some teachers called these 'learning toys and games' as distinct from those for 'playing', for example dolls' houses. Some toys were incompatible with any of the teachers' definitions of play. No classroom contained toy guns. If these were brought from home by children they were effectively confiscated. Making guns out of Leggo or other construction sets was disapproved of.

The Wendy house or home corner is an example of the constraint of provision upon play. With few exceptions I observed only variants of 'mothers and fathers' being played there. (One group of girls played 'cinemas' at the windows with dolls.) These constraints were not overwhelming since the variations were many.

> A boy tucks up a girl in 'bed'. Ties her round with ties (from the dressing-up box). Me: 'What are you playing?' Boy: 'Mothers and fathers.' Me: 'Why are you tying her up?' Boy: 'Her's dead—not really.'

Whilst it was possible for the intended use of a toy to be redefined, as when a boy used an ironing-board as a crutch, the toy often defined the play. Most collections of dressing-up clothes were of women's wear, so that boys could only dress up as women, sometimes taking the part of mother, but playing it in such a way as to singal its ridiculousness by assuming a silly voice and walk, and making much eye contact with anyone looking at them at play. After a visit from a policeman talking about road safety one class received a present of a collection of old police helmets and caps, which stimulated games of cops and robbers.

Where toys presented a number of play possibilities only certain of these were allowed. The example of making guns has already been mentioned. Children rolling the wheels of construction sets over the floor were stopped and told to 'make something'. Aeroplanes could be made, but not to drop bombs. This control of play with violent 'real-life' connotations may be seen as an attempt to maintain the definition of the children as innocent.

Children learned to share the teacher's definition of play.

> A boy in the Wendy house plays with the telephone. 'I'm going to blow this up.' Girl: 'You're not allowed to break it.'

Sometimes the definition was actively presented, as this notebook extract shows:

> Lots of rushing in and out of Wendy house. She [the teacher] leans over the top. 'Is this playing?' They [the children] look abashed. Shake heads. 'Don't be silly or else you can come out.'

The teachers also mediated the transition between play as play and play as learning. For example, a new child chose to play with a picture lotto using the cards to make houses. The next day he chose it again, but after watching him for some time the teacher approached and said, 'You like that, don't you', then asked him to find her a tree on the cards and then to put it on the tree on the board, so teaching him to play according to her definition.

Playtime

The play observed at playtimes was quite markedly different from that seen in the classrooms. The greater noise, the faster and more frequent physical movements were related to the outside location, the larger space, and larger number of children, but activities such as running chains of children, shooting imaginary guns, and fighting with invisible swords were allowed. At first sight it might be assumed that the children were defining playtime in their own way. One teacher remarked to me as we went out on playground duty, 'Now you see them in their true colours.' Certainly there were fewer constraints on the children, but their behaviour was in accord with the teachers' definition of playtime.

Most teachers viewed playtime as having a cathartic function for the children: 'let off steam', 'get the wiggles out of them'. If rain prevented the children going out in the playground, teachers often claimed they became restless and inattentive. They defined playtime to the children as a time when they could do things that they would not be allowed to do in the classroom.

'You can make as much noise as you like in the playground at playtime.'

'That's your playtime voice. We don't want it in the classroom. Save it until you go outside.'

'Jeremy, will you please behave yourself. You've had your playtime.'

To a large extent it was the teachers' definition of playtime that was allowed to prevail. This does not deny the occurrence of child generated and sustained activities contributing to the 'playground culture' described so well by Iona and Peter Opie (1958). My notes on one playtime record piggybacks in vogue, girls playing 'When Suzy was a baby', boys chanting 'Nice one, Cyril', a new game 'Spit on the seat', and intimations of serious conversations. 'Is your blood tomato sauce?' a boy asked me quite seriously. 'He [another boy] says it is.' However, all of these activities ceased almost instantly when the teacher on playground duty blew her whistle for the return to the classroom. For some teachers playtime was an awful warning of what might happen if they did not exercise control in the classroom. In the one classroom where the teacher (indirectly) admitted her lack of control, the children behaved rather as they did in the play ground (Chapter 8).

CHAPTER THREE

Other Realities—The Three R's

There can be no doubt about the primacy that all the teachers gave to what they variously called the 'basics', 'the academic side', or 'the three R's'. Whereas children could sometimes choose to paint, draw, do a jigsaw puzzle or dress up, none could refuse to read, write or do mathematics or number work when asked to do so. Sometimes they could choose when they did these things but never whether they did them. Each of these activities inducted children into worlds within the world of the classroom, into new realities.

The primacy of reading

Of the traditional three R's, reading was given paramount importance. Although clearly linked to the skill of writing, being able to read was also a prerequisite of doing much of the work in mathematics. Its importance was shown in the control exercised by the headmistresses. At Seaton Park she gave every child a reading-age test during his first year and later rechecked anyone with a low score, for progress. In the Langley school the headmistress decided when a child could proceed to the next reading book in the series. When the teacher defined the child as having read the book he or she was sent to the headmistress, who then asked the child to read a few lines before handing over the next book. Sometimes she did not agree with the teacher's definition. 'Take that back, dear, and tell your teacher you are not ready to change yet.' It is the definitions of the powerful that prevail. Two aspects of reading will be discussed: reading readiness, and the social content of what is read.

Reading readiness

The concept of reading readiness is a part of the developmental ideology.

> Is he ready to read? All children are not equally equipped to begin learning to read at a set age. (Guidance notes, Seaton Park)

If there is not a set age to start, what are the signs that children are ready to read? Teachers at Burnley Road were provided with a 31-item inventory for reading readiness.

> Concentration span: long, medium, short, non-existant (sic).
> Behaviour: settled, restless, disruptive.

Can child sit and listen well to story?
Does child enjoy looking at books quietly in reading corner?
Does child read to self or pick up a book by choice, e.g. 'choosing time'?
Does child understand that a book is a written language?
Does child know difference between a word and a picture?
Does child know what is meant by (a) a word, (b) a letter, (c) a picture?
Does child understand a word is built up of sounds?
Does child recognize same initial sound in two or three different words?
Can child hear final sound in two or three different words?
Can child sort into sets?
Can child sort and complete graded sets?
Can child complete simple puzzles?
Can child complete complex puzzles?
Can child recognize own name?
Can child write own name on own?
Can child match identical words?
Can child match identical sentences?
Can child match identical letters?
Does child have difficulty with reversals? i.e. b and d.
Does child have any other writing difficulties, i.e. mirror writing, etc.?
Can child write over teacher's words?
Can child underwrite teacher's words?
Can child copy from separate writing?
Does child attempt own writing?
Does child speak firstly to teacher (a) in class discussions, (b) privately?
Any special interests?
Does child have many friends and/or talk to other children?
Does child contribute much to class news?
Vocabulary— fluent/extensive/fair/limited

Fifty of the teachers in the general survey had new or reception children in their classes. When they were asked how they judged children to be ready for reading they generally gave only one or two criteria, which often included, 'It depends on the child', the individualism element in the ideology. Collectively their responses were very similar to those listed above, but also included some with a socialization element. 'Get them used to school first.' 'If they can't sit still for two minutes they can't start reading.' Readiness was often equated with maturity.

My observations in the classrooms suggest that individual teachers used a variety of criteria and watched for any of them to be manifested by individual children, as in this example:

Teacher holds word card up, asks named child in a group on the floor to identify the word. If the child gets it right he keeps the card. A boy hovers on the edge of the group. Teacher: 'Do you want to play?' He nods. 'Sit down.'

Whatever the sign detected it was the teacher who defined readiness. This definition was based upon externally observed behaviour which was supposed to indicate an internal mental state. I found no case where a teacher had defined a child as ready to read, and then subsequently decided the definition was wrong. Any child defined ready to read by the interpretation of any sign did read.

This child-centred basis of teaching reading is regarded as axiomatic, but millions of children learnt to read by methods that made few assumptions about the nature of the child, but placed emphasis on the nature of written language. Mitford Mathews (1966) has described the alphabetical methods used in the nineteenth century, which began with learning the alphabet, sometimes using playway methods. 'A was an Archer who shot a frog. B was a Butcher who kept a great dog.' Two-letter words were then learnt and then three-letter words leading to three-word sentences and so on.

In each school pre-reading material, such as flash cards, lead to the use of a set of reading books. These were written on a child-centred basis, the reading to fit the child.

> These 50 words [of the book] have been used to express ideas which not only are perfectly understood by small children but appeal immediately to their natural interests and sympathetic imagination . . . . (Note to Teacher, Book 1, Gay Way Series)

Since children could only read the second book having read the first, the assumption that the words and ideas of the later books could not be understood by children unless they had progressed through the earlier ones was never tested. The children's reading development was effectively defined by what they were required to read.

The multiple realities of the story world

The everyday world of the classroom was not the only one created by the teacher for presentation to the children. When children read the books provided or had books read to them by their teachers they were given access to a number of story worlds. The teachers had not written these books but in many cases they had chosen them, and so implicitly and sometimes explicitly approved of their contents. This is confirmed in their disapproving certain other kinds of books. When children brought to school annuals they had received as Christmas presents their teachers showed a polite but unenthusiastic interest, but never read from them at story time. Some expressed a rather inchoate abhorrence of these books which was often extended to comics. The Burnley Road school had a book club where children could buy books supplied by a local bookshop. The deputy head negotiated with the owner so that only approved books were on display. In a visit to a session of the book club I noticed among the Picture Puffins and Ladybird books a few Basil Brush story books. When I drew the deputy head's attention to them she said, 'Oh, I didn't see them.' She quickly gathered them up and put them behind a display stand out of sight. Some story worlds were clearly not approved.

The most obvious of the approved story worlds were those in the introductory reading books. At Burnley Road the Ladybird Series was in use throughout the school. A content analysis, including the illustrations, shows why they were approved, since the story world created by the author is in many ways similar to the classroom world that the teachers attempted to create.

The principal characters of the first nine books are Peter and Jane. They are described and illustrated as infants' teachers ideally defined young children to be. They are invariably happy, having 'fun' and 'liking' everything. Of the 429 scenes identifiable in these books 29 per cent show active or imaginative play. Peter and Jane play happily together with their friends, taking turns, sharing sweets and cakes, and are never naughty. In one picture Peter looks as though he might pull Jane's ribbon undone, but when he pours a bucket of water over her it is when they are playing in the water in their swimsuits. They are moderately adventurous but are careful to do nothing dangerous. They are kind and caring towards animals and other children, taking presents to a friend in hospital, and even their own toys for some less fortunate patients. At home they are keen to help, and are always careful to tidy up their toys before going to bed.

Peter and Jane go to school and are seen with their teachers who are talking to or supervising small groups of children, giving them interesting things to do or showing them something in a Ladybird book. However, Peter and Jane are more often seen outside school, but engaged in teacher-approved activities in contexts similar to those provided in the classroom. They have their own dressing-up box and a cupboard full of toys. They have no sandpit or water tray but they splash and play in the nearby stream and are taken on trips to the seaside. They have no playground or climbing frame but they play in the grassy garden and build Indian camps and tree houses. The house they live in is their Wendy house in that Jane does 'real' cooking in her mother's kitchen. Shopping is done in 'real' shops not the toy shops of the classroom.

The adults in Peter and Jane's world are smiling, kind, and helpful. Mother is the more prominent parent who, like the infant teacher, talks and plays with them. The bedtime story is paralleled by story time at the end of the school day, followed by teacher tucking the children into their coats, instead of their beds, until tomorrow morning.

The reading scheme used in the Langley school was the Gay Way Series. The books of this series, colour coded from red to orange, present three fairly distinct story worlds, a 'real' world of human beings, an animal–humanoid world, and the traditional story world, each, in the terms of Alfred Schutz (1967), 'a finite province of meaning'. Schutz pointed out that human beings have the capacity for living in quite different worlds of meaning. We assign different significances to an accident in the street outside our house, to a similar event on the television news, or reported in a newspaper, or part of the events in a play or novel. Schutz called these worlds of meaning multiple realities, the most intense, the paramount reality, being that of everyday life. In school this is the everyday life of the classroom. The realities of the three story worlds of the Gay Way Series correspond in different degrees to the teachers' definition of the classroom situation, but in ways that are consistent with their child-centred ideologies.

The *'real' world of human beings* is very similar to Peter and Jane's world. Ken, Pat, and Pipkin (a girl) also live in the country and own pets they care for. They are happy, kind, cooperative, and affectionate children, playing and having fun with games similar to those of Peter and Jane. The adults, too, are kindly and helpful. There is no evil in this world, and when things go wrong, as when Pipkin's doll falls out of the train window, someone puts it right—as, without a reproach, her mother recovers the doll. The developmental ideology of infant teachers is reflected in the number of stories and themes mainly concerning the youngest, Pipkin. She can only make a small snowball, she cannot be as helpful as Ken or Pat when they do the washing up, she is too small to see the ball hidden on the shed roof, 'Pipkin needs help as she is little'.

The animals in the 'real' world of human beings do not talk to one another or to people, as they do in the *animal–humanoid world*. Although not dressed as humans they are drawn in an anthropomorphic way. The dominant theme of the stories is the need for security. The animals are constantly looking for and making homes, sometimes only accomplished by cooperation. Many stories of lost kittens, chicks, and baby rabbits end in their finding their mothers (fathers are conspicuously absent). Animals can be naughty. In the first book the pig excluded from the tin pot house squashes it by sitting on it. But usually naughtiness and carelessness have their consequences; unlatched gates and unlocked doors lead to unpleasant experiences. Some animals are quite malevolent, especially the fox. Death occurs in this world. The black beetle drowns in the stew, a consequence of his foolishness in stirring it with a small spoon. His companion, the ant, briefly grieves for him, but is soon consoled by the appearance of another beetle. In 'The mouse and the flea', jokes get out of hand leading to the mouse jumping out of his skin and losing his back legs and tail.

The presentation of the animal–humanoid world as a reality distanced from that of the 'real' world, mitigates the assumed effects that descriptions of macabre mutilations, evil, and death may have upon the vulnerable innocence of children. Such things are presumed less 'real', and therefore less upsetting than they would be in the world of Pipkin. Even the versions of the traditional stories are presented in their less brutal variants: all of the three little pigs survive, and the small and middle size billy goats escape the troll.

In the 'real' world of humans, conventional reality is largely preserved. In the animal–humanoid world it is modified by the replacement of humans by animals. Human beings, when they rarely appear, do not communicate with animals. In the *traditional story world* humans, animals, plants, and objects speak to one another. Magic transformations are possible. Events are unpredictable. They are not always the logical consequences of actions but are due to luck, spells or bad fortune.

The 'real' world of Pipkin is wholly good, and apart from the bad foxes and trolls the animal–humanoid is also good; misfortune only follows foolishness. In the traditional story world all reality is rather slippery, and morality is less clearly defined. A common theme, as in 'The animals' winter hut', is the necessity to stick together in a wicked and unpredictable world. The child reader is protected from harm by the distancing of this story world away from the everyday life idealized in the 'real' world stories. The 'unreality' of magic, of talking animals and objects, is part of this, and the humans are not dressed in contemporary styles but in the usual middle-European medieval peasant dress of the traditional story world. In addition, these stories only occur in the later books of the series, to be read by older children.

This analysis and speculative interpretation of the multiple realities of the story world concerns only the meanings of the teachers. No imputations are made of the orientation of the authors, although W. Murray, author of the Ladybird Series, is described as a lecturer and headmaster, and E. R. Boyce, author of the Gay Way Series, has also written several books on infant education, so that both have the status of 'experts' in this field. Nor is any imputation made about the meanings that children assign to the experiences of reading these stories or of having others read to them. Sometimes it appeared to teachers that some children had not properly defined the story world as a different order of reality. A boy's mother reported he had nightmares after hearing his teacher read the story of Daedalus and Icarus. In telling me about it the teacher said, 'And I did tell them it was only a story.'

Writing, news and stories—the reproduction of realities

Learning to read and learning to write were closely connected. Writing skills were used as indices of reading readiness, reading skills were tested by the use of written exercises. A fairly common sequence of learning to write began with the child having her name written on her drawing by the teacher. The child then either copied it or traced over its pencilled outline in crayon. Children's pictures were used in the next stage.

> Teacher to child: 'Tell me about your picture.' Child: 'It's a flower.' 'It's a very lovely flower, where is it?' 'In my garden.' Teacher writes under the picture, 'Here is a flower in my garden.'

Such 'stories' were either copied or traced, and eventually became more the child's composition. Children never achieved complete autonomy in their writing. They were dependent on the teacher's definition of how words were spelt (often collected in their word books or 'dictionaries'), and whether it was sufficient.

> Teacher reading last sentence of boy's story. 'They lived happily ever after.' 'Go on, they had nowhere to live. Go and write about it.'

Teachers defined acceptable grammar.

> 'Not, "It is windows in the castle". What you should say is, "It has windows", or "There are windows".'

They also defined acceptable topics. 'I'm tired of war stories.'

Three kinds of writing activities were followed by the older child: exercises, news, and story. A typical work card exercise was to copy and complete the writing on the card.

> Look here, Peter says.
> Look here, he s———.
> The fish can jump.
> ———, the f——— can j———!

The writing of news often followed a talking session about things the children had done over the weekend. Even here the children could not define whether something had happened to them, because their teachers were concerned that they ordered the reality of news separately from that of story.

> 'If it were your story book you could tell me you've been in a Red Arrow, but you've not actually been in a Red Arrow—this is your newsbook.' (*N.B.* Red Arrows are an aircraft display team.)

News was supposed to relate to the 'real world' and to orthodox reality, similar to that of the real-life stories in their reading books.

> 'Where did you go to see rabbits flying about?'

Writing stories was intended to give children the opportunity for imaginative expression, but, as the following transcript of a tape-recording shows, teachers' definitions were still important.

TEACHER: Now the rest of you are going to write stories. Come close to me and listen. Same book. Come along to your places. Now are you listening? Stories! Close your eyes and feel them. Think what your story is going to be about. First of all it's going to be your own special story. No one else's will be quite like yours because yours will be special. What's it going to be about, think! Shut your eyes. Might be about a wicked old, horrid, old witch. Yes, it might be about a dainty little fairy just all in silver and gold and pretty colours. It might be about a nasty, fierce monster, it might be about a big, big, big, tall giant. It might be about a little mouse with a little, little tail. Little curly tail. Might be about a rabbit with a little white bobtail. Or a dolls' house where a little family of dolls live. Might be a bedroom, bathroom, sitting-room, kitchen. I wonder who lives in the house. Well you'll all have to write about it, won't you? It might be a story about a penny that rolled and rolled and rolled away, and I wonder where it went. Well you'll all have to tell me, won't you. Might be about a dinosaur, those prehistoric animals who lived long, long ago. It might be a story about a prince or a princess. Shut your eyes please. Don't talk! Your own special story. Just yours. O.K. What's yours going to be. Yes?
PUPIL: A dinosaur.
TEACHER: A dinosaur.
PUPIL: A naughty boy.
TEACHER: Your story is going to be about a naughty boy.
PUPIL: A tramp.
TEACHER: Nobody has written a story about a tramp. You'll be the first one.
PUPIL: A witch.
TEACHER: A witch, yes.
TEACHER: Yes, you know there are hundreds and hundreds of other things that stories could be about. Could be a ghost, couldn't it? Could be about all sorts of things.

Twenty-one children wrote stories. Five had a witch theme, four were about dinosaurs, two about princesses, and one each about a rabbit, a prince, a mouse, and a penny. Thus 15 of the 21 stories were related to the teacher's suggestions. The remaining themes were Dracula, artist, park-keeper, naughty bike, dragon, and a tramp. Earlier the same morning there had been a class discussion about the jobs people do, when both artist and park-keeper were mentioned, but not

Dracula. Clearly the teacher had contributed to almost every child's 'own special story'.

However, children could create their own story worlds where conventional reality did not have to prevail, and which corresponded to the animal–humanoid and traditional story worlds of the reading books. Writing reproduced these realities.

> Once upon a time there was a cat and it had kittens it had five kittens one was called ping one was pong and the other three were called Dong Wong and Song one day mother cat took Dong and Wong to the shops and she bought some toys and they lived happily ever after

> Once upon a time there was a princess and she was called Jane and one day she went out to meet her father and a witch peeped round the corer and got her and her mother saw it and Janes father came home and he saw the witch killing her and the king killd the witch and then he got Jane and he toke her home with him and put her in bed and made her better

Some children quite clearly drew upon non-school sources of inspiration.

> Once upon a time there was a dark dark castle and in the castle there is a grave and in the grave there is a skeleton of Dracula. and one day someone went inside the castle creek went the door as he crept in and his name was Frank Drake and then he found a wooden stick it was called the stake and he stuck it in the grave and the skeleton. came alive who are you said Frank Drake I am Dracula and tonight i thirst and just then a lady came in and Dracula changed into a vampire and flew over and sucked some blood out of the lady.

Later in the day the teacher read some of the stories aloud to the class including the one about a park-keeper. However, as the following shows, she did not read out what the boy had written. He wrote:

> Once upon a time there was a park keeper one-day he was piking up some rubbish and a giant he piked him up and took him to his catle and locked him up the giant had some wine and some food, then he went to bed the park keeper died and in the morning he played his harp.

She read:

> Once upon a time there was a park-keeper. One day he was picking up some rubbish and a giant he picked him up and took him to his castle and locked him up. The giant had some wine and some food then he went to bed and in the morning he played his harp.

Her omission of the death of the park-keeper was only noticed some time later when the story and tape transcript were compared, and so I did not have the opportunity to discuss this with her. I can only speculate that the omission was due to the story's mixing of the usually discrete 'real-life' and traditional story worlds. Death was only acceptable in the latter, at a safe and non-upsetting distance from innocent children. Books were read to children where the story worlds were mixed, for example Sendak's *Where the Wild Things Are* (1970), about a boy and fantastic monsters, or Zolotow's *Mr. Rabbit and the Lovely Present* (1968), where a girl is in serious conversation with a rabbit, but the real-life human never comes to harm.

Number and mathematics—the suspension of orthodox reality

The teachers' distinction between number work and mathematics was not a clear-cut one. Learning to count and computations involving the four functions were often called number work or old-fashioned sums, but these were also included in some teachers' definitions of mathematics. All teachers defined mathematics as including the kind of activities associated with the series of work-books *Mathematics for Schools*, known after their senior author as Fletcher books. Children were sometimes told to get on with their Fletcher. *Mathematics for Schools* was used in every class of the Langley and Seaton Park schools, and although the children at Burnley Road did not use the work books they were provided with material, mainly work cards and sheets, that their teachers had derived from the Fletcher books.

The teachers did not regard themselves as possessing a specialized body of knowledge to be transmitted to their pupils. They were experts in arranging for children to learn. Writing and reading and basic number work were regarded as skills that most adults possessed in some degree. Mathematics was not defined in this way. It was regarded as being slightly esoteric. This was the only classroom activity that some teachers confessed to not quite fully understanding themselves. Their acceptance of the Fletcher books was partly an acknowledgement of the authority of the headmistress in deciding this part of the curriculum, but also their implicit acceptance of the expert authority of the authors.

The expert tone of the series is set by the Foreword by Professor W. H. Cockcroft, endorsing 'guides to good mathematics teaching', and the senior author, Harold Fletcher, a senior inspector in mathematics. The introduction to the series neatly fuses the expert authority on the nature of mathematics and expert authority on the nature of the child. The methods used are posed as congruent with the child-centred ideologies of infant education.

> Its aim to inspire children by giving them a lively sense of *interest* and *pleasure* in mathematics and its *creative* use in everyday living.
>
> . . . we have given careful consideration to the courses of all mathematical *experiences* and the logical and *psychological* processes involved, from the reception class upward . . . .
>
> . . . the study of mathematics is to *free* children rather than inhibit them.
>
> . . . help you plan a *happy*, modern, *progressive* and integrated mathematics course . . . .
>
> Given time and an opportunity to respond in accordance with *maturity*, the vast majority of children can succeed. (From, 'Understand the Series' and 'Using the Series')

I have italicized the key words in this fusion of external, expert authority and the teachers' professional ideologies. To these can be added references to discovery-activity and mathematical development. There is even a concept of mathematical readiness and a warning against rush tactics. Teachers using the books implicitly accepted the authors' definition of the fit between the nature of mathematical concepts and the child's development, and the definition was real in its consequences, in that no child was allowed to work through Book 2 before completing Book 1, or, for example, to learn how to tell the time before learning how to measure length.

The Fletcher world of mathematics has a superficial resemblance to the 'real-life' world presented to children in some of the stories they read, and which they may have reproduced in their writing. The illustrations are similar, showing children, animals, food, tools, toys, aeroplanes, and cards. A few of these even hint of the animal–humanoid world, such an anthropomorphized smiling snail and a cat with a bow tie. However, in the world of mathematics conventional reality may be suspended.

Sharon does maths work book. She follows the instructions to colour some dolls blue and some red. 'I've never seen people with blue or red faces', she says, mainly to herself.

A boy sorts sets using plastic shapes including yellow Scottie dogs, orange pigs, yellow horses, and purple elephants.

At the Langley school the Fletcher books were supplemented by Hume and Wheeler's *My First Book of Sums* which contains pictures of orange-coloured apples, pears, bananas, lemons, and grapefruit. As I will describe in the following chapter, such aberrations were likely to be commented upon by teachers if drawn by children.

The mathematical basis of the Fletcher scheme is the concept of the set, referring to things the same in one or more respects, for example colour or shape. Most children encounter the set in relation to a collection of things to be used together, for example nurse's set, train set, tea set. 'Real-life' objects may be involved in mathematics but 'real-life' meanings must sometimes be suspended.

Mathematics was 'done' in work-books, and also as practical exercises, initially defined as play, including measuring dimensions, weights, and volumes. These activities were considered to be part of the concept-building process and also an expression of the purposeful nature of mathematics 'in that it deals with people and life'. However, practical mathematics transmuted the 'real-life' world into the reality of mathematics. A class exercise on measuring height or counting eye colour became a histogram. Marbles, acorns, shells, fingers, and other counters became figures on page, objects became numbers.

Children learnt to count by repeating numbers after the teacher, but beyond this stage the skills of reading and to some extent writing were also involved. In following the Fletcher scheme or teacher-prepared work cards children were presented with phrases such as, 'Partition the set in different ways', and 'Complete the number sentences'. Most teachers were aware that younger children could not read the instructions properly but suggested they 'know how to do it [the mathematics] without it'. When reading as a part of 'reading' or when writing as a part of 'writing', pupils were expected to recognize each word read or written. In mathematics words could be left meaningless. This deliberate or allowed creation of situations which kept the children ignorant is a form of what Pierre Bourdieu (1977) has called symbolic violence, and it was particular to their mathematical education.

The Burnley Road and Seaton Park schools had maths workshops where some mathematics sessions took place. Their existence was an index of the special nature of mathematics. They were stores of resources, such as balances and rulers, and their walls were covered in pupils' project material and displays prepared by the teachers. One of the latter had the title, 'A tesselation of triangles and dodecagons'. The teacher who had prepared it admitted that she did not expect any child to be able to read it. It is possible that this created ignorance was recognized and allowed by the teachers because of their own orientation towards mathematics as somewhat esoteric knowledge.

One consequence of this situation was that teachers controlled the pace at which children worked through the Fletcher books, since often only they could read the instructions. Another was that for some children doing elementary mathematics was mainly a colouring exercise.

A girl is doing her Fletcher. I ask her to read the instructions at the top of the page. She says, 'Colour the cars.' They read, 'Ring round the sets having the same colour.'

This could lead to their completing the task 'properly' and therefore appearing to have learnt what they were intended to learn—but not always.

There are pictures of six hens. The instructions say, 'Colour then join.' She colours two hens yellow, two blue, and two green, and joins them by colour into three pairs. The intention of the exercise is to create a set of six birds of any colour.

The multiple realities of the classroom

Teachers defined the reality of every day life in their classrooms. Within this they also created other orders of reality, the story worlds of reading, the writing worlds of news and story, and the world of number and mathematics. Children learnt to share their teachers' definitions of the nature of these provinces of meaning by reproducing them in their reading aloud, in their writing, and in doing sums or problems. They also learnt which of these worlds they inhabited at a given time. Pink elephants may exist in one of the story worlds or the world of mathematics, but never in the 'real-life' world of news or of Peter and Jane, or, as the next chapter shows, in a 'proper' painting or drawing.

CHAPTER FOUR

Creativity and Conventional Reality

Drawing, painting, sewing, collage, and model-making were all common activities in the classrooms, in that all children did some of these things during the course of the day. Sometimes they were organized around a theme or class project based upon the children's imputed interests, and at certain times of the year they were directed towards special public occasions, such as the Harvest Festival or Christmas Concert. Although apparently free and expressive, these creative efforts were constrained by the actions of the teachers, who defined them in terms of the presumed developmental capacities of the children, and the consequences of this definition were shown in the products of the children's activities. Creative work was also partly organized to reproduce conventional or orthodox reality, a process given greater priority, for different reasons, when the products were to be publicly presented.

Painting and drawing—reproducing conventional reality

Every day every child probably did a drawing or drawings. These were sometimes parts of mathematical or number activities, the prelude or accompaniment to a story. The drawing of pictures was also used by teachers as a way of sustaining busyness, to be done in spare moments on pieces of paper or in busy books. This kind of drawing activity was common among the younger children, who, to begin with, were allowed to make their own definition of a drawing.

> Teacher looking at girl's drawing: 'I like it, what is it?'

Paintings, too, could be defined by the younger children.

> Teacher introduces the new boy (his second day in school) to painting. He is shown the easel, the paints, the brushes, and the apron he must wear, but he is not told how or what to paint. He uses one colour to cover most of the paper. Another boy says to him, 'What are you painting?' He replies, 'A colour.' The other boy, 'A colour, just blue!' He changes brushes and completes the painting in green.

The boy had defined painting as covering a surface with paint.

In the absence of the teacher defining a drawing or painting, young children learnt from one another; a whole table frequently did the same basic drawing by copying. The familiar images were those of houses, trees, and flowers. These were seen by some teachers as expressions of the children's needs for security, a therapeutic introduction to school, and a few of the younger ones drew on the authority of 'what they told us at college' to support this. The college orthodoxy also forbade asking what a picture was of.

The representations of houses, trees, flowers, and people were versions of cultural images of these things. Although not directly presented to children by the teachers these were displayed in the classroom, other than in other children's paintings and drawings. Lollipop trees and houses based on a rectangle and a triangle were found on Leggo cards, teacher-prepared and commercial word and number cards, mathematics work books, and in some story books.

Left to define paintings for themselves the children drew on the limited resources around them, but to the teacher their limited images were an indication of the limited resources within them: their relative immaturity. I tried a simple, ethically acceptable, experiment one day. A boy was about to paint. I asked him what he was going to do. 'I don't know.' I suggested, 'Why don't you paint a boat?' The teacher was quite excited when she asked him her usual question, 'Tell me about your picture', and he replied, 'It's a boat'. 'He's never done anything like that before,' she said to me later. At least three other children, following his example, 'progressed' to painting boats that day.

These early drawings and paintings were defined by the teachers as expressions of childish innocence.

Teacher, looking at boy's painting: 'Cubist. I suppose he'll lose all that soon.'

Children were emancipated from their innocence by the actions of their teachers. After a period in which they could paint or draw what they wished, older children's images were monitored by the teacher's comments so as to introduce more elements of conventional reality.

Teacher: 'Where's the door on your house?' Girl: 'Hasn't got one.' Teacher: 'How do you get in?'

'Poor daddy! He hasn't got any arms.'

These comment sometimes denied the children the ability to express perspective.

The girl's picture has a house and a girl of the same height. Teacher: 'I like the girl and the house, but could she get in the door?'

The conventional reality that the children were required to represent was often more a conventional picture reality.

A group are making collage trees from squares of sticky paper. Teacher: 'Have you ever seen a black tree trunk?' 'You're not doing a green tree trunk are you?' No trees outside the window have the chocolate brown trunks that she requires. Some are shades of green, others almost black, and even white.

This conventional picture reality was used in the learning of colours.

There is a 'blue' display of pictures prepared by the teacher, including ones labelled 'The sea is blue', 'The sky is blue'. Outside the sky is grey. It can be red, purple, orange, yellow, or white.

Children learnt to reproduce these picture realities.

Girl, of another's painting: 'Sky don't go that colour.' (Green)

Some children presented token representations of picture reality. It was common to observe a child to first paint a blue line along the top of the paper to represent the sky, and then a green one at the bottom for grass. Teachers did not find this acceptable in the paintings of older children, and asked for a 'proper' sky that stretched down to the horizon.

Teachers also constrained children into the reproduction of conventional reality by their provision of materials.

> Children are making collage fruits and vegetables from sticky paper. 'Cabbage people, here are yours' (two shades of green). 'Tomato people, these are yours' (red).

Teachers used children's painting and drawings as an index of their developmental state or maturity. An internal state inferred from an external product mediated by the teacher.

> We are looking at the afternoon's picture work on the 'sea' project. The teacher makes judgements of the children's maturity: 'They haven't got the concepts to draw properly yet.' The drawings of the less mature children are less detailed, the heads are large, there is no perspective. She is delighted with a boy's picture of a diver. 'He has come on.' She is nonplussed when I tell her I saw him copy it minutely from a Ladybird book.

Public display—the effort/product dilemma

Teachers defined children's creative work as being an expression of their development, and acted in such a way as to make the nature of their creative products correspond to the presumed stages of development. In this the teacher judged the children, but when their products were on public display the teachers felt that they too were being judged. This was tacit acknowledgement of the teacher's part in the creative process, and one which, when I had gained their confidence, they were prepared to admit.

The classrooms were public places to the extent that they were visited by other teachers, the headteacher, and parents delivering and collecting their young children. Children's paintings and drawings were displayed on the walls, often mounted on coloured paper with a teacher-provided caption. 'This is Darren's daddy.' The three schools held Open Days for parents and on these occasions the classrooms were more than usually decked with creative work. Some of the captions were clearly for the benefit of the parents: 'Some collage pictures', 'Splatter painting', 'Wax-resist paintings'. On these occasions it was possible to see how the teacher had sometimes strengthened the outline on a child's picture or even added some detail.

At Seaton Park and Burnley Road every teacher had a turn at taking prayers. This was a performance put on by one class in front of the rest of the school, and typically involved the display of children's creative work. At Seaton Park this was put into a public area of the school for a period after the prayers. Taking prayers was a minor ordeal for the younger teachers. 'This is where the butterflies start,' said one as we walked to the hall for her first performance. Afterwards she was sympathetically congratulated by her colleagues (even though she forgot to do the closing prayer).

Each performance was arranged around a theme or story such as 'growing up' or 'things we like to do'. Rehearsals and the production of material often started weeks before the performance. The latter presented the teachers with a dilemma. Left to create their own efforts the children would produce elephants and giraffes that did not look much like elephants and giraffes. To use these would be to evaluate the effort over the product. Most teachers intervened to make the product correspond better to conventional reality; the product was evaluated over the children's efforts. Many argued that the children enjoyed contributing to making a recognizable product. For others this was a compromise with their professional ideologies and a source of conflict.

> Mrs Pink's class project for prayers is 'Ourselves'. For this each child is doing a self-portrait on the reverse side of a continuous roll of wallpaper to make a 'mural'. She is concerned on two accounts. Firstly, the children are clearly copying the previous portrait in doing their own. She feels they should really be drawing themselves, so she covers over the previous portraits (with great difficulty because some are still wet). She is then, secondly, concerned to find that some children are drawing bodiless figures with the arms and legs attached to the head. She compromises 'as it's for assembly', and unrolls the paper so that the previous acceptable figures can be copied. She feels guilty about this as 'they should find out about people having bodies for themselves'. Later she even mediates verbally. 'He's something missing.' Other children chorus, 'Arms.'

In the production of work for public display the teacher was the designer and the children routine workers. One teacher said quite explicitly, 'They are the manual labourers.' Their labour included their (happily) filling in outlines prepared by the teacher, for example an elephant of paper clips and an owl of different kinds of seeds, the mass production of leaves and fish from templates prepared by the teacher, and the assembly of parts to make angels or Easter cards. In these efforts it was the teacher who was being creative, and as a later section shows the quality of her class's work was one way in which she was evaluated by her colleagues and the headmistress (Chapter 8).

There were, however, observable incidents of genuine creativity by children.

> A boy finds an old record in the junk box. He makes a record-player from a cornflakes packet, a cotton reel, and rolled-up corrugated paper. He moves the record around by hand on the cornflakes packet and sings, 'I'm a long-haired lover from Liverpool'.

Projects and imputed interests

Many of the activities that the teachers arranged for children to do were based upon their imputations of children's interests.

> We must start from the natural interests of the children. (Notes for teachers, Seaton Park)

Teachers made assumptions about children's interest in providing books, reading stories, and in starting off projects which stimulated the children's interest, so proving the original assumptions to be 'real'. They were assumed to be interested in animals, flowers, people's jobs, cars and trains, singing, poetry, and royalty. 'They are all royalists,' said one teacher to me at the end of a day when she had used Princess Anne's wedding as a topic at news time, having previously asked them to bring in newspaper cuttings of the event, displayed a portrait of the wedding couple from a women's magazine framed in flattened milk bottle tops, got every child to do a picture of the event, and set the older ones to write about it.

Boy: 'Can I do [a painting of] Princess Anne?' Teacher: 'If you want to.' Boy to another, excitedly: 'I'm going to do Princess Anne.' Later he does his writing. 'I like Princess Anne. I like Captain Mark Phillips.' The names are written on the board. I look back in his writing book. Yesterday he wrote, 'I like swets and is lolly.' The day before, 'I like dogs.'

This is not to suggest that children's interests were totally teacher-stimulated.

Girls chatting as they work: 'My mum says Princess Anne's veil was the Queen's.'

However, some manifest interests of children were not given educational status by their teachers.

It is singing time. The teacher asks the children to choose the songs. After 'Mary Mary quite contrary' and 'Little bird' a boy suggests 'I'll be your long-haired lover from Liverpool'. The teacher says, 'No, we're not having that, we don't all know the words.' She ignores the many children who call out, 'I do, I do.' 'No, we'll have Humpty Dumpty.'

The only pop songs that children sang were at least 20 years old, such as 'How much is that doggy in the window?'. Other interests of the children that were ignored included most television programmes, a frequent topic of conversation among children in the classroom, comics, and anything to do with fighting, death or wars, unless these were safely set in a historical context (the Vikings comprise the major part of infant history), or, in a story world setting, particularly pirates. The following overheard snatches illustrate children's non-approved interests.

Boy: 'Who likes Scooby-Doo?' 'Me!' chorus the children around him. They sing a snatch of the Scooby-Doo song.

Children are swapping horror stories in the Wendy house. 'My dad has a bit cut off the end of his finger.' 'My friend's dad had half his tongue cut off.'

Non-approved interests also appeared in the children's writing, despite teachers' oblique disapproval. ('Not another war story.')

One day there was a man half monster and they called him Francken Stein and one day when superman looked and a saw people coming upstairs so he got in to decgiese clark kent and he and he saw Francken Stien and killed him.

One day there was a boy called Dennis the mennis and when he was eating his dinner he said it was horribel and he chucked his dinner in his mums face so she got daddy and daddy smaked his head and told him.

Disapproved and unutilized interests were those which contradicted the teacher's definition of the pupils as being innocent and those that related to orders of reality, including television programmes, which were outside her control.

CHAPTER FIVE

Teachers Teaching—Children Learning?

The index of the Plowden Report contains 34 references to learning, but not one to teaching. In the classroom it was usually easier to recognize that the teacher was teaching, than to be sure that the children were learning or what they had learnt. When the teacher had been manifestly teaching she usually assessed how much the children had learnt: manifest learning. However, the assessment of learning did not always follow teaching. Some learning occurred independently of the teacher's activities, and in some cases was possibly unintended and even unrecognized by her.

Manifest teaching—manifest learning

Manifest teaching and manifest learning were most closely associated with the three R's. Flash cards were used throughout the stages of teaching and learning to read. A common procedure was for the teacher to hold up a picture, ask any or a particular child to identify it, and then present a second card with the name of the identified object. Sometimes she would be more didactic and simply display the word card saying what it meant, first making the children repeat, and then later identify the word. Sometimes this manifest teaching was done by a teacher-surrogate, an older more fluent child with a group of beginners. At other times children worked in pairs, each acting as both teacher and learner.

> The first boy holds up the flash card to present the obverse side with the word 'nest' to the second boy. The reverse side seen by the first boy has a picture of a nest. The second boy says, 'Nest.' The first boy turns over the card to show he is correct. It is then the second boy's turn to be teacher.

In this example both boys could be learning, whether they were presenting or identifying the card. Children also learnt to read from one another in the group flash-card work. Without answering they could learn from other children's correct and incorrect answers.

Flash-card preparation led to the act of reading to the teacher. If the preparation had been adequate the child could identify all or most of the words in that part of the book, and so could 'read' a few pages. When a word could not be identified then the teacher taught it, sometimes directly, or sometimes obliquely, mouthing it or pronouncing the first syllable. In this situation the children read the teacher's face not the book. Sometimes the teacher tried to 'coax' the word out. In fact she was teaching it obliquely.

> The boy cannot identify 'mother'. The teacher prompts him. 'Come on, it begins with an um sound.' 'Mum?' he guesses. 'Sometimes you say mum. Sometimes you say mummy but when you get a bit more grown up you say . . .?' He gets it: 'Mother!'

> The boy reads 'now' for 'how'. Teacher: 'Not now. If you were a Red Indian you'd come up to me, put your hand up like this and say . . .?' Unfortunately he doesn't know the conventional greeting of Red Indians.

Most teachers tried to hear the beginners read every day, but this aim was sometimes not achieved, because 'there are so many other things to do'. The time given to hearing individual children read was often quite short. During one period of observation the average was 73 seconds. Teachers usually did other things at the same time as hearing reading. On one occasion during the course of hearing one child read a teacher tied another child's shoe-lace, urged several others on with their work, wrote words in word books, but at no time looked at the book the child was reading from. She, and others I asked, explained that she knew the book 'backwards', and could hear the child despite all that was going on. However, on several occasions I heard children miss out words or get words wrong which the teacher either ignored or did not hear.

With older children the teachers' main concern was less that they recognized words but that they understood the meaning of what they had read. Teachers used two ways of assessing this. They sometimes asked questions about the story, and they also listened to the candence and expression of the reading. Reading line by line rather than by clause or sentence was taken to be indicative of imperfect understanding.

Reading activities were the reproduction of teacher-defined meanings. Writing, too, was an act of reproducing such meanings, as well as being the reproduction of teacher-defined orders of reality, already discussed (Chapter 3). As previous sections have shown, the manifest teaching of writing was often associated with that of reading, and being able to read was often demonstrated by being able to write, as in the exercises involving the completion of sentences.

Doing sums or mathematical exercises were also acts of reproducing teacher definitions as a part of mathematical reality; 2 and 2 may only make 4, and a square must have four equal sides and an internal right angle. The manifest teaching of number was often straightforwardly didactic. Individuals or groups were asked to count aloud. As with the early stages of reading the children learnt from one another. Careful listening often revealed that a handful of children were saying their numbers fractionally before all the others; when they made a mistake, so did the others. On one occasion I observed a girl 'counting' in the same way as the famous 'talking' horse, Clever Hans.

> Teacher asks Denise to count off six on the number cards pinned to the wall. She looks at the teacher not the cards, placing a finger on each card, following the teacher's nods and smiles; she pauses at five but goes on to six with a few more signals, which then stop, and so does she.

Previous descriptions have shown that the learning of number and mathematics involved writing and reading, but that not everything that was presented to be read was expected to be understood (Chapter 3). Three other examples of this symbolic violence were observed, where children were deliberately kept in a state of ignorance; these were doing handwriting, 'Time and Tune', and learning songs.

Children first learnt to print but later were taught joined writing. The methods including tracing over writing prepared by the teacher, copying from the board, and copying from handwriting texts such as the *English Writing Books* by Ruth Fagg. On several occasions I asked children to read what they were copying from these books; at most they could only recognize a few words. When I discussed this with teachers they accepted my observation, but said it did not matter since the point of the exercise was not to read but to learn handwriting.

Most classes listened to the B.B.C. radio programmes 'Time and Tune', and in many cases older children were given the 'Time and Tune' books. Whilst they could sometimes read the words of the songs, few, if any, could understand the musical notation which was also printed. However, most of the teachers were also ignorant in this respect. This implied that musical knowledge had a special, esoteric status. Musically literate teachers, especially the few pianists, were given a special status among colleagues, often receiving a higher-scale post on this account. In the general survey several of the small infants' schools were without pianists, a situation defined as a serious problem by the headteachers.

Many of the simple songs sung in the classroom, such as 'Five penny buns' and 'Tommy Thumb', were fairly obviously understood by the children, but the songs sung at prayers and on special occasions like the Christmas Concert sometimes were not. Listening carefully to the children singing I could hear them using the wrong words, sometimes neologisms. Teachers were aware of this and sometimes spoke with amusement of these mistakes. The second line of 'All things bright and beautiful' was sung as 'All teachers great and small'. The children were taught these songs in a purely rote fashion, and teachers seldom explained either the general meaning or particular words, in this case obviously including 'creatures'. The teachers' main concern was the tone of the singing. Children were asked to sing 'nicely', 'sweetly', with 'soft voices, please', perhaps to conform with conventional ideas of childish innocence. The children obviously enjoyed singing these sometimes meaningless songs, perhaps sufficient justification in itself, although they appeared to prefer to use their open, lusty, non-approved voices.

Some of the pupil learning was not intended by the teachers, including the songs, games, and lore transmitted from child to child in the playground (Chapter 2). Teachers recognized that this sort of learning took place but were not always aware that elements of this child culture were brought into the classroom. Unlike me they could not 'disappear' to overhear this kind of jokey exchange:

Boy to girl: 'There's a hole in the armpit of your jacket, you feel.' She does. 'Only monkeys do that.' Girl: 'Only maltesers do that!'

Incidental and polyphasic teaching

Manifest teaching of the basic skills took place in discrete or designated periods of time. Incidental teaching was more adventitious, usually shorter in duration, and sometimes used to plug gaps of time, such as waiting for the dinner ladies to arrive, and to maintain busyness. As one teacher put it, 'We never miss an opportunity.' Collecting dinner money was often the opportunity for a class exercise in counting, addition, and the calendar. Incidental teaching was often combined with the incidental assessment of learning.

> The teacher has been doing flash cards. She allows the children to keep those they have correctly identified. 'How many have you got?' she asks each. They count. 'Then you are first, you are second, and who is third?'

Manifest teaching often included incidental teaching as a secondary element and so was polyphasic teaching. Approved behaviour and politeness was often taught in this way.

> Teacher: 'No, not Fursday, we must put our tongue out a little bit. Thursday. It's the only time we can do it without being rude.'

Sometimes in polyphasic teaching the incidental elements were more numerous than the manifest purpose, as in this example, cooking.

> TEACHER: What must you do before you do any cooking?
> CHILDREN: Roll up your sleeves and wash your hands.
> TEACHER: Right, girls go first.
> The boys put on green-striped aprons, the girls flowery ones. The teacher goes through the ingredients. 'We need four ounces of sugar.' She points to 4 on the scales. 'We could use butter but we'll use margarine. It's just as good and it's cheaper than butter.' The mixing stage is reached. 'Now who's going to have first go? We'll have someone who didn't shout out.'

Apart from being taught how to make a sponge cake the children were being taught hygiene, sex differentiation, numbers, food economics, and politeness. Some of the children may have learnt these, some may have known already. In some cases of incidental teaching it was difficult to know whether and what the children had learnt since the teacher did not assess their learning.

Sometimes it was difficult to judge whether the things teachers said to children were intended to be teaching acts: they seemed so incidental as to be unintended. Did the teacher who said, 'We'll have to keep our fingers crossed and see what happens', intend to transmit this conventional superstition? When I asked her she could not remember saying it. A boy found a snail in the wet sandbox. The teacher took the opportunity for some adventitious teaching. She drew the children's attention to its 'horns' and 'the little house on its back'. When a girl went to touch it she said, 'Ug, don't touch it, it's all slimy. One of the boys, pick it up and put it outside.' Did she intend to transmit the message that snails are nasty things not fit for little girls to touch? Did the children learn this or did they know it already?

Everyday knowledge

Although a few children started school with some knowledge of how to read, write, and count, teachers assumed that all pupils had to acquire these skills, and that they were expert in bringing this about. Many of the other activities in the classroom were concerned with what might be called everyday knowledge, the cultural equipment that teachers assumed all children should have. They sometimes transmitted this directly, but more commonly assumed that at least some of the children had this knowledge and arranged situations in which this was publicly demonstrated and therefore potentially shared by all the children.

In the following example, a transcript of a tape-recording, the teacher had all the children sitting around her on the floor and had pinned up a picture (from *Child Education Quarterly*) of a christening, the class project being Festivals.

TEACHER:	What is the matter, John? You know what he's doing?
PUPILS:	(Inaudible)
TEACHER:	Listen one at a time. Listen one at a time. John, you tell us what he's doing.
JOHN:	Making a cross on his hand.
TEACHER:	What is he doing? What is it? What is it that's in the picture? What is it called?
PUPIL:	He is being christened.
TEACHER:	He is being christened. What happens when you're christened?
PUPIL:	You get a name
TEACHER:	You get your name. What's your name?
PUPIL:	Davin.
TEACHER:	Davin. Where do you think this is taken from? Who do you think they are?
PUPIL:	From the church.
TEACHER:	In a church. What makes you think it's a church?
PUPILS:	(Inaudible)
TEACHER:	Wait! Listen one at a time shall we? Steven?
STEVEN:	And you have christening cake.
TEACHER:	And you have christening cake. Where do you have christening cake. In church?
PUPILS:	No.
TEACHER:	When do you have christening cake? At home? Afterwards or before?
PUPILS:	Afterwards.
TEACHER:	Afterwards. What do we call this here?
PUPIL:	I know.
TEACHER:	What is it?
PUPIL:	A font.
TEACHER:	A font. That's a good boy, Sean. That's a font! That's a font. Who do you think we've got here? Look.
PUPILS:	People.
TEACHER:	Yes, people. What particular people? Martin?
MARTIN:	(Inaudible) . . . old-fashioned people.
TEACHER:	Pardon?
MARTIN:	Old-fashioned people.
TEACHER:	Old-fashioned people. Well, do you think they belong to the baby?
PUPILS:	No.
TEACHER:	Fiona?
FIONA:	Yes, they do.

TEACHER:	You think that they belong to the baby. Who do you think they are, then, these people down here?
PUPIL:	They're the family.
TEACHER:	They're the family! Who do you think is here? Who do you think this is here?
PUPILS:	Mummy.
TEACHER:	You think that this is the mummy. And who do you think this is here?
PUPILS:	The daddy.
TEACHER:	Who do you think this is here?
PUPILS:	An uncle.
TEACHER:	Uncle or grandad, I should think. Who do you think these people are here? Who? Who?
PUPILS:	The cousins.
TEACHER:	Some people that are special people that have to go to a christening. Can anybody tell me what they are called? Special people that have to go to a . . . Karina?
KRINA:	Cousins.
TEACHER:	Yes, well, cousins would go well but you have special people at your christening.
PUPIL:	Nannies.
TEACHER:	Nannies come, yes!
PUPIL:	Parents.
TEACHER:	Yes, parents come but someone else very special.
PUPIL:	Cousins.
TEACHER:	Yes, we said cousins, Martin.
PUPIL:	The christening man.
TEACHER:	Oh yes, children!
PUPIL:	And christening man.
TEACHER:	What do you call the christening man?
PUPIL:	A vicar.
TEACHER:	A vicar. That's right! That's the christening man. Who do you think these other people are? Do you have somebody special to a, to a christening? Rena. You've been to a christening.
RENA:	Your auntie and your nannie.
TEACHER:	Yes aunties and nannies come.
RENA:	And uncles!
TEACHER:	And uncles, yes!
TEACHER:	Some special people come as well. GODPARENTS! If it's a little boy.
PUPIL:	(Inaudible)
TEACHER:	That's right, they go to look after you, aren't they? Do you think that this is a little boy or a little girl?
PUPILS:	A boy, a little boy!
PUPIL:	A little girl!
TEACHER:	Well, we don't know do we? But if it is a little boy he has two grandfathers and one grandmother. No! I said grandmother, didn't I? Godmother and two godfathers. If it's a little girl she has two godmothers. There you are. So that's perhaps what they are, then, the godparents! The godmothers and the godfathers. Joanna?
JOANNA:	I've been to a christening with my auntie but it wasn't their house, it was another house and we had lovely teas.
TEACHER:	Lovely teas, yes. Now Karina?
KARINA:	When you sometimes you got to a christening you can see which is a boy and a girl cause a boy a girl has a long dress and um a boy has a short dress.
TEACHER:	Either a short a dress or a a little short suit. What colour do we say for a boy as a rule?

PUPIL:	White.
PUPIL:	Blue.
TEACHER:	Blue for a boy and what for a girl?
PUPILS:	White.
PUPIL:	Green! Green!
TEACHER:	White or?
PUPILS:	Pink.
TEACHER:	Pink! Pink! That's right.

I discussed the recording with the teacher (and similar tapes with other teachers) and she confirmed the following conscious and purposeful elements. She did not want to tell the children about christenings, she assumed that some would know something about them and used the picture to elicit the initial response and structure the process. When a child gave the 'correct' knowledge the teacher repeated it for emphasis. (Christened, vicar.) Where a child gave the 'wrong' answer it was generally ignored. ('Incorrect' colours for boys/girls.) Children's contributions that lead away from the theme were not followed up. (Christening tea.) The teacher only transmitted the knowledge when it seemed that no child knew it. (Godparents.) At the end of the 'chat' she assumed the children 'knew about christenings'. Thus the culture of everyday life was learnt and shared.

Teacher ignorance

The teachers regarded themselves as experts in arranging for children to learn. Children learnt skills and things that 'everyone knows' or, perhaps, ought to know. Teachers did not define themselves as experts holding a body of knowledge to be transmitted to the children. Some were rather scornful of 'facts' as having no place in a child-centred education. ('Facts' did not include two and two make four, or c a t spells cat.)

Nature study and science were supposed by the headteachers to be part of the curriculum. Some of the former could be observed, but little of the latter. Science was largely confined to magnets and magnifying glasses, or as one child called them 'magnetfying glasses'. His explanation (to me) of the magnet was also a play on words: magnets picked up things 'by magnic'. Many teachers, too, appeared ignorant of orthodox scientific facts and explanations.

Teacher, taking a 'movement' theme assembly: 'Butterflies have no legs. Caterpillars crawl like worms and snakes.' Second teacher, following up the assembly in class: 'Butterflies have no legs to walk with.'

Sometimes the apparent ignorance may have been explained by the teacher simplifying things for younger children. Thus, birds had noses, an owl consisted of 'tummy, arms, beak, and feet'. At other times teachers would accept the children's definitions which were incorrect by scientific orthodoxy.

Teacher: 'What's the different between a turtle and a tortoise?' Girl: 'Tortoise got all squares on it.' 'That's right.'

Sometimes it seemed that either the teachers were careless of the 'facts' and explanations or just ignorant of them.

'An alligator is a big kind of crocodile.' 'A crocodile is just a big alligator.' (Same teacher, different occasions.)

Teacher, following up a television programme about Holland: 'A windmill blows the wind around.' 'What does a windmill do?' Boy: 'Pumps electric.' 'Good boy. Yes, windmills can be worked by electricity.'

On one of the few occasions when I judged it acceptable to refer to this kind of 'mistake', the teacher said, 'I don't think it matters so long as you give them some kind of explanation.' Sometimes the ignorance was scarcely of a scientific order.

Teacher, summarizing a discussion: 'Yes, a cockerel goes cock-a-doodle-doo. A cockerel is a man or boy hen. A chicken is a girl or lady one.'

The headteachers were only concerned about some of the teachers' ignorance of orthodox spelling. Among the howlers I saw on prominent display were 'daffodill' and 'robbin'.

CHAPTER SIX

Social Control in the Classroom

As a stranger to infants' classrooms I found it difficult to make sense of all the activities I saw in my earliest observation periods. After a number of visits I began to see a pattern or order to events which was similar in most classrooms. This social order of the classroom was created and maintained by the teacher's exercise of social control. Social control involves the use of power. Weber (1964) defined power as 'the chance of a man or a number of men to realize their own will in a communal action even against the resistance of others who are participating in the action'. The definition may be rephrased to fit the classroom situation. 'Power is the chance of a teacher realizing her own will in classroom activities against the resistance of the children.' The will of most teachers was realized in the classroom situation. There was order to their general satisfaction, their definition of the classroom situation was made real. In these terms, power is the chance of the teacher's definition of the classroom situation being made real against the resistance of the children.

However, there was little evidence of children resisting in this way. Weber (1964) called the willing compliance to power, legitimation, and legitimized power he called authority. Most children most of the time acknowledged the authority of the teachers. The basis of this legitimacy was difficult to discover. The research by Jean Jones and Basil Bernstein showed that mothers do prepare their children for the prospect of school, and this may include defining the teacher as a person with authority. My observations were that children may also learn to acknowledge the authority of the teacher from other children. In each school children were received into the reception classes either individually or in small groups. With a few exceptions these were mixed-age classes, so that new children entered a group all of whom had previous experience of the classroom and the teacher. From the teacher's point of view these arrangements were advantageous in 'getting them settled in quickly' or, in different terms, their accepting her authority and definition of the situation.

I observed Tina on her first day at the Seaton Park school. She was the only newcomer that day and was brought by her mother half an hour after school started, and when the rest of the class were already busy. The teacher immediately gave her a piece of paper to draw on, and kept 'an eye on her' for most of the day. Tina looked around a great deal at the other children, and from time to time caught the eye of the teacher. At milk time she finished her crisps last of all. She ran to the teacher: 'I've finished my crisps.' 'O.K., my dear, put the bag over there.' They listened to a story on record. Tina said something to a girl close to her. 'Do you know this story, Tina?' Tina nodded to the teacher's question. During singing time she did not join in the clapping at the teacher's signal, but after she had seen the other children clap. She took her drawing to the teacher, having seen others do so, and received her approval: 'Very nice.' Throughout the day Tina's experience was that the teacher commented upon her actions and told her what to do. Furthermore, she saw most of the other children being treated in the same way and generally responding to the teacher's requests. The authority of the teacher was demonstrated, as was its acceptance by the other children, and she accepted it too. When I asked children why they were doing something they usually said, 'Because teacher told me to.'

'Schools' was quite a common game played by younger children in the classroom. In this the teacher–pupil relationship was very strongly one of dominance and subordination, 'teachers' often hectoring and bullying the 'pupils' in ways unlike anything they themselves experienced in school. This draconian play-definition of the teacher may have had its origins outside of the school, perhaps with their parents' reports of their experience of school in an earlier historical period. It could be part of the cultural image of the teacher as an authority figure. Even in the Ladybird readers when the children play at school, the 'teacher' wears glasses, a gown, mortarboard, and holds a long stick.

Weber's definition of power refers to the 'chance' of someone realizing their will against the resistance of others. The chances were high for teachers to realize their will, but sometimes an individual child could effectively resist. David brought his own book to school and was pleased to have it read by the teacher. Later she asked him three times to clear up his table. In a temper he tore up his book. His teacher decided not to stop him because, as she told me later, she thought she couldn't. Later he knocked over a display on the nature table which the teacher chose to ignore. The next day she ignored a number of other incidents for fear of another 'tantrum'. At playtime he insisted he didn't want to go out. She saved the situation by saying, 'All right, David, you can stay in and tidy up.' For a few days it was his definition that prevailed and the real consequence was that the teacher did what he wanted her to.

The chance element in the exercise of power means that all forms of social control are slightly tenuous. For most teachers this was not a serious problem, even though they were responsible for thirty or more children carrying out many different activities in a classroom stocked with many things, and where the potential for chaos was enormous. Even in doing music and movement or P.E. they felt their control to be quite secure. However, their view of its slightly tenuous, even mysterious, nature was shown in their difficulty in explaining why although everything went as they wanted it to most of the time, sometimes, without their obviously doing anything different, their expectations were not met. They posed several 'theories' to explain the 'off days'. 'It's either me or some of them got out of the wrong side today.' Weather theories were very common. Wind was supposed to make the children excitable. Rain, which kept them in at playtime, made them restless. Cold kept them quiet.

Methods of social control

The arrangements that teachers made for the learning of reading, writing, number, and mathematics, for the doing of projects and craft work were all forms of social control. This social control of learning was exercised together with the control of behaviour: what was sometimes called by the headmistresses 'class management', although, interestingly, none of them included this in her notes for teachers. As previous examples have shown, the control of learning and the control of behaviour were often exercised together in the same situation. For example, it was not enough for a child to give the right answer, it had to be given in the right way.

Teacher: 'I heard what you said but you didn't put your hand up.'

Teachers exercised control of behaviour in two circumstances: adventitiously as the situation required, 'Someone is being silly', or in anticipation of a situation, 'Now we are going to the hall and we must be very quiet going down the corridor'. Teachers used a large number of methods of control; some were common to most teachers, others were quite idiosyncratic. Some appeared to be more effective than others. Most were consonant with the teachers' recipe ideologies of child-centredness.

Their methods of control were typically *oblique*, particularly with younger children. Their preference was to make requests rather than to give orders, to reward good behaviour rather than punish the bad. These actions were consonant with the idea of the children being innocent. They were capable of being naughty but did not have naughty intentions. When I put this analysis to teachers they confirmed it with phrases like, 'Well yes, you can't really blame them, can you.'

Two methods commonly used by teachers were also successful ones in terms of the teachers' satisfaction with the outcome of their use, and my observations of the consequences in the pupils' behaviour. These were the use of eye-scanning and contact, and the use of public and private voices.

Eye-scanning and contact was described by teachers as 'keeping an eye on them'. This required the teacher being able to see all the children, and so the furniture was arranged to eliminate any obvious blind spots. This was easy when she chose to receive children and their work at her table, but less so when she chose to move around to their tables to assess and explain. Whatever she was doing, she would from time to time scan the class with a look, particularly if some noise or movement caught her attention. The children would also from time to time look at her, particularly if they had done something of which they thought she might disapprove. Sometimes this was the guilty, give-away look. This visual control was often unaccompanied by words.

The boy knocks over a jar of pencils on to the floor. He looks at the teacher. She looks at him. He picks up the pencils.

The use of scanning implied the omniscience of the teacher over classroom events—she saw everything.

The same boys knocks over the same jar of pencils. He looks at the teacher. She seems not to have seen the incident. He pauses and then picks them up.

This attempt to project omniscience, or 'with-it-ness' in the phrase of Jacob Kounin (1970), was made quite explicit by the teachers.

'Well you just can't afford to take your eyes off them, can you? There's no telling what they will be up to. You have to let them know you know what they are doing.'

My observations show how the newer pupils learnt to look at the teacher by looking at the others looking at her. They learnt to interpret the teacher's *facial expression*, how to react to a smile with a smile, an enquiring look with an explanation, an aggrieved, sad look with downcast eyes, an I've-seen-you-do-it look with an end to the disapproved behaviour.

Public and private voices were used by most teachers. The private voice was directed towards a single child or small group close to her, and was only audible to them. I had to gain the teacher's confidence before I could get close enough to hear too. Fortunately many used their public voice a great deal. Although not loud it could be heard in all parts of the classroom, even when the teacher used it to address a single child. As with eye-scanning, the public voice established her presence everywhere, above the 'busy hum', into the blind spots of the book corner and Wendy house. The consequence of its use was that when behaviour was approved or disapproved it was posed as applying to all the children. It was common to see several children tidying up after one child had been either praised for being tidy or reproved for being untidy. This was also another indirect method of teaching.

Teacher, marking boy's sums: 'Didn't you remember to put the date at the top?' On the other side of the room a whole table of children hastily put the date on their sum sheets.

A similar 'ripple effect', as Kounin (1970) calls it, could be seen when teachers made an unspecified comment.

'There's one little girl who is being very quiet and hardworking.'

'There's three people not working I can see.'

The children learnt to interpret the various *teacher voices*. I detected five with distinctive tone, delivery, accompanying facial expression, and meanings above those of the phrases actually spoken:

'Now we are going to do something exciting' voice;
'Slightly aggrieved, sad' voice;
'I'm being very patient with you' voice;
'Oh, never mind, don't let's have a fuss' voice;
'Listen to me, I'm saying something important' voice.

Most of the forms of verbal control used with younger children were oblique. Three sorts of phrases were very common:

Thinking or wishing aloud. 'I hope nobody is going to spoil our lovely story.'

The no-need-to-answer question. 'Are you getting on with your work?' to someone obviously not doing so.

Sometimes these amounted to *silly questions*. 'I hope you are not making a mess again', when confronted by a conspicuous mess.

The more direct equivalents of these phrases, 'Don't spoil the story', 'Get on with your work', 'You've made a mess again', were less common, and used only with older children. Obliqueness was also part of the way children were sometimes addressed. 'Is Daren getting his book out today?' Not, 'Daren, are you getting your book out today?'

The oblique nature of the control was also shown in the teachers' use of pronouns.

Teacher: 'When everyone is ready *we* will choose someone to bring in the milk.'

She chose the someone. To use the more correct 'I' would have been too direct.

Oblique control was shown in the teachers' avoidance of telling younger children directly that their work was incorrect. With sums it was 'Two to check' rather than 'Two wrong'. 'I write a "p" this way' to a boy who had written it "q".

Reference control was used when some external authority was evoked.

'Put the apron on. What would Mummy say if you come home with paint on that nice new jumper?'

Headteacher reference control was sometimes used.

'Now, nice and quietly down the corridor. You know Mrs Brown does not like noisy children.'

The headmistresses knew they were used as 'bogies' and did not like it. Their authority over both children and teachers was demonstrated in the way they could stop or redirect activities when they came into a classroom, their involvement in the reading programme already referred to, and their part in assembly or prayers. At the Langley school the headmistress always led the assembly. At Burnley Road it opened with 'Good morning Mrs Brown, good morning everyone'. The class 'prayers' were implicitly offered to her, and at the end she thanked them. Perhaps there was even a fusion of sacred and secular authority in a way similar to that I had observed in secondary schools (1973). 'Prayers' was posed as something special.

The class is going in to prayers. Teacher, to boy laughing and talking loudly: 'Shssh. Remember where you're going.'

Several teachers admitted that they used a spoken grace before milk time as a control device, and going home prayers were 'a nice way to finish, and gets them quiet and calmed down'. Calling the register was a 'good way of getting them started'.

Make-a-game-of-it control drew upon learning through play.

Teacher must leave the children in the hall during music and movement. 'I won't be long. I want you to curl up on the floor and go to sleep like little dormice.'

'Boys close eyes. Girls creep out, quietly get your coats. Don't let the boys hear you!'

An extension of this was what the headmistress of the Langley school called 'tricks', to be used when things were getting a little out of hand.

> Lets have a stretch. Wiggle fingers. Big yawn. Hands on heads. Fingers on lips. Lock hands in laps.

Control by *joking* was sometimes used, but little in the form of sarcasm or irony.

> 'Don't put your finger in there Mark [the chair strut], it will get fixed and we'll have to bring your tea here to you.'

Sometimes the joke could be *shaming*.

> A boy sucks his thumb. Teacher: 'Darren isn't singing today. He has a chocolate thumb.' Some children laugh. Darren does not.

Most methods of social control were strongly dependent on the context for an understanding of their meaning. This was so in the use of *naming*. 'David' could mean a number of things: stop doing that, get on with what you are supposed to be doing, come here. The use of first name and surname, 'David Stedden', signalled strong disapproval. The use of adult titles, 'Now Miss', 'Come along, Mr Stedden', signalled mild, but sometimes amused, disapproval. Children smiled when addressed in this way.

Some idiosyncratic forms of verbal control could be highly condensed. Many teachers had their own particular words, for example, 'Chattering' (said very slowly). One teacher was in the habit of prefacing her speech with 'Er'. In the appropriate context, 'Er' could quickly reduce the noise to a busy hum. Similarly, holding teacher's hand or sitting near her could be either a reward or a punishment, well recognized by the children.

Isolation and *distraction* were also used.

> Vanessa is being silly in the corner. 'Vanessa, will you put these crayons away for me?'

This is also a good example of the *request–command*. Most threats were *idle threats*, but they were effective.

> 'If you don't hurry up you won't have any playtime.'

Appeals were usually directed to individual children rather than the whole class.

> Teacher kneels and grasps Gary by the forearms. She looks into his eyes and talks about 9 inches away from his face and says in a private voice, 'Now I want you to be a good boy and do your writing. Will you do that for me?' He nods.

In the general survey of teachers they were asked how they dealt with the 'naughty ones'. Distraction was mentioned by 9 per cent, appeals also by 9 per cent, deprivations by 17 per cent, isolation by 29 per cent, and verbal methods by 41 per cent. After they replied to that question we asked them, 'Do you ever smack them?', and 47 per cent said they did. Many modified their response by stressing its infrequency, 'About three times in ten years', and its lightness, 'Just a tap on the legs—not really a smack'.

I saw a few cases of *smacking* and most of them were tokens, but not always.

The smacking incident happened very quickly. Mrs Pink moved swiftly and surely to the mat where the boys were playing, and smacked Brian on the hand. He is near to tears. In discussing the incident with her later she explained it in terms of what he did then and what he had done earlier that day. In the morning she had asked who wanted to go to the toilet. He had not gone and later wet his pants. This involved the infants' helper coming in with a loan of some clean ones. At the time of the smacking he was playing with some new big Lego pieces. The children had been previously warned that they must be careful not to break them. He broke some trying to separate the pieces by banging them on the floor.

In this incident Brian's actions were not judged to be innocent.

Classroom rules

Social control was exercised to create order according to rules propagated by the teachers. These rules were sometimes explicit but more often implicit. Most were consonant with the teacher's ideologies so that there was a continuity between the forms of child-centred social control and the order that they were used to maintain.

In my first efforts to understand the nature of the order the teachers were trying to attain I began to hear them using pairs of words in a dichotomized way. The most obvious was silly/sensible. Children's action or children themselves were often labelled, disapprovingly, silly or, approvingly, sensible. Some actions were nearly always silly or sensible. These were verbally indicated in other word pairs again applied to actions or children. These were explicitly tidy/untidy, quiet/noisy, busy/lazy. The word polite was often used but its opposite, rude, was usually only implied. 'Helpful' was common but not 'unhelpful'. Sensible 'nice' and 'kind' were common, silly 'nasty' and 'unkind' uncommon. Both halves of the more powerful good/naughty were in frequent use, but in general there were more approving utterances than disapproving ones. The children were more often encouraged and rewarded for being or doing things that were sensible, good, kind, tidy, quiet, busy, helpful, polite, and nice than they were discouraged or sanctioned for being or doing things that were silly, unkind, naughty, untidy, noisy or lazy. Some of the connections between these paired word-judgements are shown in the following examples:

'Now I can see the *sensible* people because they are *busy* working already.'

'Go into prayers *quietly* and *sensibly*, sing as *nicely* as you can.'

'I want Paul to sit by me because he has been so *nice* and *helpful*.'

'Gary you are being *silly* and *noisy*. No I'm not smiling. I'm sorry.'

Approved and disapproved behaviour were sometimes expressed in idiosyncratic labels for pupils: tidy pilers (of books), Womble helpers, sensible choosers (of games), Mr or Miss Chatterbox, horrid shouters.

Sometimes approved behaviour was explicitly formulated as rules or principles.

'You can talk all day but you must be quiet at story time.'

'We can't work and talk at the same time.'

'Kind hands don't grab and snatch, they share.'

Teachers would often test the children's knowledge of these rules either to reprove them or to ensure their being followed in the near future.

TEACHER: Who is going to run down the corridor?
CHILDREN: Nobody.

TEACHER: Now tell me, there is one thing I don't like—what is it?
CHILDREN: Noise.

TEACHER: What must we do when we've finished painting?
CHILDREN: Wash our hands.

The premium on *tidiness* was clearly based on the potential for untidiness in classrooms full of materials with children engaged in many different activities. Many methods were used to maintain tidiness; tidying by rota, tidying for teacher, tidying a privilege (rewarded by staying in at breaktime to tidy), tidying a punishment (punished by staying in at breaktime to tidy), tidying by bustle ('Jonathan, there's a piece of puzzle by your chair. Pick it up, please. Sarah there's a crayon over there. Tina . . .'). The alternative was, teacher tidies up after school.

Politeness was sometimes expressed in rules or principles.

'You must answer me when I ask you something.'
'Don't say what, say pardon.'

'If you are nicely mannered people are always pleased to help you.'

Or established through questioning:

BOY: Can I go toilet?
TEACHER: Pardon? (She has heard what he said.)

BOY: Can I go toilet, please.
TEACHER: Just remember those two very special words.
CHILDREN: (in chorus) Please and thank you.

Rules and principles of behaviour were concerned with teacher–pupil and pupil–pupil relations, but children were not allowed to draw the teacher's attention to another's infringements. *Tell-tales* were not listened to. This was partly to preserve elements of childish innocence, but it also preserved the status of the teacher as the moral authority in the classroom.

GIRL: Gary keeps flicking paint on my picture.
TEACHER: I'm sure he didn't mean to.

Teachers could express approval or disapproval of either an act or an individual. Approval of either the act or the individual was effective in that the recipient was pleased and other children copied the approved act. Disapproving of an action was associated with the recipient looking upset or shamed, but disapproval of the individual appeared more upsetting and more permanent, and less effective in that the disapproved behaviour was often repeated. In terms of the maintenance of order it was better for teachers to label naughty behaviour rather than naughty children. To point out naughty behaviour was to pose a norm that applied to all children; being a naughty child was an individual property.

I observed that teachers who were most content with the effectiveness of their control had two characteristics. Firstly, they made their expectations and rules quite explicit. This refers to both work tasks and behaviour. Secondly, they used a great deal of approval and praise when the expectations were met and the rules kept. Their rare use of disapproval was more effective than the disapproval of those teachers who used it much in sanctioning the failure to meet expectations or for breaking the rules. The children had an infinite appetite for approval; the taste of disapproval did not seem much worse with frequent doses. Interestingly, these observations have been confirmed experimentally by Madsen and his associates (1968).

In a few classrooms I saw what amounted to operant conditioning. Teachers did not make their expectations at all clear but rewarded the surprised children when they did the right thing by accident.

Classroom rules were used to enable children to engage in activities in ways that were acceptable to their teachers. However, these rules did not hold equally for all children. Another pair of words I frequently heard the teachers use were big/little, referring to children. In the mixed-age classroom the older, 'big' children were expected to be more sensible, tidy, quiet, busy, polite, and nice. They were defined as having developed to a more mature stage and the definition was real in its consequences; they were more often sanctioned if they were, silly, untidy or noisy. The 'little ones' were defined as more innocent and were consequently not expected to keep the rules in the same way.

'Stop what you are doing please, now. Terry, why did you walk after I said stop? You are one of the biggest in the class and you know you should stop. Tracey, you moved but you are new.' (Doing P. E.)

'John, you're not really helping me, and I'm surprised at you because you are one of the older boys.'

Out of control

The maintenance of order by the exercise of social control was accomplished to most teachers' satisfaction most of the time, in the ways I have described. In each of the three schools there was one teacher whom the headmistress defined as not having things under control. At Seaton Park and the Langley school these were teachers in their probation year, and the headmistresses asked me not to observe them. Mrs White was in her third year of teaching. She had failed her probationary year but had 'passed' after a further year. Implicitly, she agreed with the headmistress, Mrs Brown, that her class was not well controlled.

'I'm afraid they're not like Mrs Pink's children.'

'They can be quiet sometimes.'

'Haven't you had enough?' (When I asked to return for a second visit.)

She agreed to my observing in her classroom. Much of the time the children behaved as if they were in the playground. Mrs White used very little public voice but even when she shouted they took little notice of her. She used little eye-gaze and the children seldom looked at her. Getting them ready for P.E. or to go home took a long time and she was sometimes reduced to physically pushing and even lifting children about. Several children took no notice of her requests or orders and she ignored their ignoring. On several occasions children went missing from the room.

Mrs White's colleagues were quietly sympathetic towards her. To them she was a reminder of the necessity for effective social control and of the fragile nature of the social order of the classroom. In Mrs White's classroom it was the pupils who had most power to define the situation. Mrs White left the school and teaching the following year.

CHAPTER SEVEN

'Building Pictures'—The Assessment and Typification of Children

The children spent most of their time with one teacher—their teacher. Depending on staff turnover and the headmistress's policy, a given child could be with the same teacher for as long as two years. During this time she would 'get to know' her children, and by the teachers' own accounts they took about half a term to 'build up a picture' of each one. Schutz (1932, 1972) called this process of making sense of social experience 'typification'. Each teacher constructed typifications of each of her children which were part of her personal stock of classroom knowledge. Intimations of these were apparent in the use of a public voice in the exercise of control.

'There's always some silly person who spoils things, Alan.'

'Thank you, Linda. The only kind person.'

Sometimes when we were discussing a particular incident the teacher would describe her picture of the child concerned. These typifications were the way the children were to the teacher. They were her definitions of what was real about each child.

It would not have been possible for me to elicit and record all of the teachers' typifications of all of the pupils, more than a thousand altogether in the three schools. However, after my periods of observation in each school the headmistress gave me permission to look at the records kept about each child. These were written by the teachers and were to some degree formalized versions of their typifications of individual pupils, and therefore form a third source, together with public utterances and private verbal accounts.

The processes of typification were inseparable from those of assessing the work and behaviour of individual children. I have already described how assessment was integral to the processes of teaching and learning, and how much of the exercise of control was based upon judgements of children's behaviour. Typification, assessment, teaching, learning, controlling, and being controlled were all aspects of the same flow of action and interaction in the classroom, and they were all consonant with the teachers' recipe ideologies, particularly those of development and individuality. Although individual teachers typified and assessed particular children, the nature of their typifications and assessments was similar because of their common, shared bases—the institutionalized recipe ideologies of child-centred education.

The assessment and typification of individual children

The processes of assessment and typification started straight away. At the end of Tina's first day at school I asked her teacher, Mrs Sadler, if she had any immediate impressions, and how she had formed them. She thought that Tina could be 'quite bright'. She had done a painting with recognizable objects, and when asked by Mrs Sadler had said she had not done painting before. She had copied some words Mrs Sadler had written on her drawing 'quite well', and had shown she could write her own name. In her relations with other children she seemed self-possessed and 'not easily bossed', 'a little bouncy', and Mrs Sadler thought she could be 'a bit of a nuisance'. However, she stressed that 'they often change after the first few days'. A week later Mrs Sadler reported that Tina had cried rather unexpectedly when another new child did, and had been visibly reluctant to leave her mother in the mornings. At the end of the term, Mrs Sadler described Tina as being 'bright enough', on the basis of her progress in reading, no longer 'shy' of school, but 'willing to try anything new'.

This example illustrates three important points about the way teachers assessed and typified pupils. Firstly, they drew mainly upon their own experience of the child in the classroom situation. Other teachers' written records of some of the older children were available, but were seldom consulted. Usually they were only looked at towards the end of the school year in the process of bringing them up to date. Children were a common topic of conversation in the staff-room, but 'no one knows my children like I do, even if they did take them last year'. Secondly, three aspects of each child's classroom behaviour were assessed and

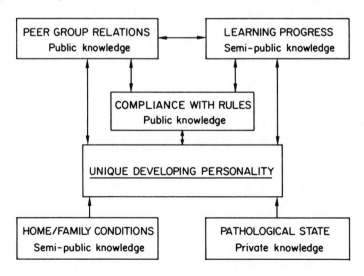

Figure 1 Teachers' typifications of individual children

incorporated into the picture or typification: compliance with the teacher's rules of behaviour, relationships with other children, and their learning progress. Thirdly, the typifications were not absolute, but varied over time.

From my various sources, observations, teachers talking about children, and their written records, I was able to analyse the process of typification from the teacher's point of view as follows:

> Each child possesses a unique, developing personality, which is expressed in his or her compliance with classroom rules, relationships with other children, and learning progress, each of which may influence the others. Children change naturally as they develop, but changes may also be due to changes in home or family circumstances, or illness.

This is summarized in Figure 1. This also indicates how some knowledge of the various elements and of the teacher's assessments was known publicly by the children in the class, but much was kept private by the teacher, including the typifications of individual children she used the knowledge to construct.

The assessment of compliance with classroom rules

Teachers created rules to maintain order in the classroom. The exercise of social control in relation to those rules involved making assessments of children's behaviour. Children knew they were being assessed and the teacher's assessments were often made public in the act of exercising even oblique control.

> 'Someone's being silly.'

Individual pupils could be publicly typified as well or badly behaved:

> 'As usual we have Daren playing around.'

The Newbridge Education Authority's infants' school record card required teachers' estimates for each child's 'conduct'. The headmistresses did not like the cards, and did not use them entirely according to the authority's instructions. Mrs Baker of Seaton Park supplemented them with a record system of her own, as did Miss Fox of the Langley school, but less elaborately. All three heads allowed teachers to leave parts of the cards blank. I have already mentioned that the teachers seldom referred to the records of older children. The headmistresses suspected that the headmasters of the junior (later middle) schools did not make much use of them either, when they were sent with the children at the time of transfer. Mrs Baker was upset to discover that her middle school counterpart had actually destroyed the detailed files she had sent to him soon after receiving them. I suspect that, like those in the infants' schools, other teachers prefer to judge children on the basis of first-hand experience, rather than written, often dated, records. This evaluation may explain why I found, to the headmistresses' surprise, that the records were often far from complete.

The most complete records were at the Langley school. In the conduct assessment the teachers rated their children on a three-part scale, A good, B satisfactory, C poor. In addition they wrote a short description of each child so that I was able to infer what counted as 'good' and 'poor' behaviour, and how the well- and poorly-behaved children were typified. Not surprisingly the words written by the teachers were similar to those they used in controlling the children in the classroom (Chapter 6). The silly/sensible distinction was used in 11 per cent of the notes, and quiet/noisy in 21 per cent. As in the classroom the assessment took into account the child's presumed maturation; the big/little verbal distinction became the mature/immature distinction, used in 10 per cent of cases. Thus the A, or well-behaved child, was quiet, sensible, and mature; the C, or badly-behaved child, was noisy, silly, and immature.

In the classrooms teachers expressed more approval of behaviour than disapproval, and generally felt secure in their control. At the Langley school 12 of the 16 teachers gave more As for conduct than either Bs or Cs, and no one gave more Cs than As or Bs. The overall distribution was A 49.6 per cent, B 32.8 per cent, and C 17.6 per cent. (Total number 415.) In each class about half the children were typified as well behaved, and only a handful were 'naughty' in their behaviour, but in their immaturity they were not usually naughty in intent.

Teachers regarded classroom behaviour as one expression of a child's unique personality.

Lively but obedient.

Mature, confident, sensible, tries hard to please.

Sly, sometimes quietly naughty.

The assessment of relations with other pupils

The 'conduct' assessment sometimes included comments on how the child related to others in the class. The children knew of these relationships, who was friends with whom, but did not know that their teacher assessed them in terms of these relationships; the knowledge was public but the assessment private. The importance of this assessment was shown in a special category 'socialization' in the 'progress' record book designed by Mrs Baker at Seaton Park. Teachers generally expressed favour towards being popular and being able to make friends easily. Concern was expressed about children who preferred their own company, and were therefore thought not to be happy and settled in school.

Happy, mixes well.

Worrying, tends to be an isolate.

Teachers regarded a child's peer-group relations as an expression of his or her unique personality.

Quiet and shy, no special friends.

Silly, excitable, a bit spiteful to others.

Peer-group relations were sometimes thought to have consequences for compliance with classroom rules.

Pleasant reliable child but can be influenced by others to her detriment.

Easily led. Sometimes influenced by other boys' behaviour.

The assessment of learning progress

Assessment was integral to the processes of learning to read and doing mathematics. 'Progress' was indicated by which book or card a child had reached, and appeared in the written records. Individual children knew which book they had reached, and although teachers often privately congratulated children when they moved on to a new book, this was not made obviously public. In the general survey of teachers most of them (80 per cent) reported the use of reading groups. My observations show that in practice such groups were used mainly for preparatory flash-card work and had an effective existence for only a few minutes each day. Often they were not identified as groups. The teacher would just call out some names. In some of the more structured forms of integrated day they were identified, often colour coded, but not just as reading groups, but for other activities as well including, sometimes, playing.

The criterion used in the creation of reading groups was reading 'level', 'progress' or 'ability'. The terms were used singly or together and with the same operational definition; children were grouped by the book they were reading at that time. The use of the term 'ability' may be thought to imply the teachers' acceptance of what Geoffrey Esland (1971) has called the psychometric model of the child's capacity to learn. This is the institutionalized ideology of the normal curve, or what Bernstein *et al.* (1966) have called the substance model of intelligence: a few children have a lot of intelligence, most an average amount, and a few have a little. However, most infants' teachers fairly clearly disavowed this view. In talking about learning groups they were insistent on the flexibility of their composition, which my observations confirm. They were changed 'frequently', 'all the time', 'any time', 'from day to day'. Children were sometimes moved to produce 'amenable groups' that got on well together, but mainly because of their 'progress'.

'I change them if they progress or fall back.'

'If one suddenly spurts and another slows down then I change them around.'

'Some moved as they develop.'

'If the children progress at different rates then the groups are naturally changed.'

'Groups have roughly the same level of maturity.'

This was not the psychometric model of children's ability but a developmental one.

'Groups are individuals who happen to be at the same stage.

Children's capacity to learn varied according to the level of their development which could be erratic and unpredictable, 'spurting' and 'slowing'. For this reason the meaning of the group was kept from them, and they were not told why they were moved from group to group.

'They don't know why they're changed. There's no point in upsetting them.'

The teachers seldom spoke of intelligence or intelligent children. In the written records of the three schools I found only one use of intelligence as a description of a child. Its nearest equivalent was 'interested' or 'keen', used in 15 per cent of the records at the Langley school, but this referred to disposition rather than capacity. Teachers did describe children to me as 'slow' or 'bright' but, as with 'interested', 'bright' was a disposition rather than a capacity. The record card did not require an assessment of ability but of 'attitude to work'. Eleven out of 16 teachers at the Langley school gave more A ratings than either B or C. Overall 51.1 per cent were rated A, 30.1 per cent B, and 18.8 per cent C: not a normal curve but skewed towards the bright or favourable.

Some acceptance of the psychometric model was shown by some of the teachers of the older children, particularly after the reorganization to form first schools keeping the children until they were eight. One teacher of rising eights appointed from a junior school said she thought of them in terms of 'the old A, B, and C streams'. Only one teacher of reception children expressed the psychometric model of ability. Perhaps, significantly, she too was junior and not infant trained. Unusually she had a complete class of reception children. After a term she created four reading groups by 'ability', a small group of the 'cleverest', two bigger groups for the 'average', and a small group of the 'slower ones'. I asked her how she detected 'ability'.

'It's difficult to say really but I could tell who was going to do well after about a week. It's something to do with the way they look and take an interest in things. They are more grown up really, not so babyish.'

However, like her colleagues, she kept these assessments private, and did not use the terms 'bright', 'clever', 'average' or 'slow' in the classroom.

A child's learning progress was another expression of his or her unique developing personality.

Immature, easily distracted, lacks concentration.

Withdrawn, reluctant to try new work.

Immature, silly, loses interest.

David has some emotional problems and often appears anxious. He produces work of a good standard but I feel he is under-achieving at times.

Sometimes a child's progress was related to his general behaviour in terms of compliance with classroom rules.

He has made very little progress in school and seeks to be the cause of much trouble and small disturbances amongst other children because of immaturity.

Peer-group relations were also judged to be associated with progress.

Lacks concentration in a group but works well on own.

She has learnt to trust her own abilities more and has become more relaxed with other children.

Changing typifications

Teachers frequently redrew their pictures of children. They observed changes in behaviour, in relations with others and in rates of progress, and consequently changed their typifications. The most important explanation made of these changes was that they were natural and developmental.

> He is going through a silly phase at the moment.

> More mature and sensible, behaviour much improved, was rather a lone child but now mixes well.

> Tracy was a very quiet girl when she started school, she would only speak when spoken to and needed directing in everything she did. She has become more integrated with the class, has many friends and enjoys being 'bossy' in the Wendy house.

> Settled, work has matured.

> Conscientious work, gradually gaining confidence in herself.

> Jane has made remarkable progress in reading since entering the school. She is changing from a very shy and self-effacing little girl into a more extravert and independent one.

Changes that were judged as favourable were defined as natural and developmental. Those judged as unfavourable were explained in terms of factors which could not be blamed on the innocent child: illness or disability, and home or family circumstances. Teachers learnt of children's health problems through their absence and subsequent notes from parents, directly from the parents when returning the child or at parents' meetings, from the child himself, and sometimes from medical reports which the headmistresses received and made a point of drawing to the attention of the teacher. Such knowledge was kept private and was used to explain changes and deficiencies in behaviour, relationships and progress.

> Reliable but lacks confidence probably as a result of the appearance of her skin complaint.

> A quiet child who gets on well with other children but doesn't like big groups. Unsure of himself because of speech difficulties. Attends speech therapy at school.

> He has been in hospital recently for tests for a suspected duodenal ulcer. He can be very aggressive with little provocation.

Information about changing home circumstances was sometimes given by parents to the headteachers or teachers; it was also available from the children. Child-centred methods gave plenty of opportunities for this. Children painted 'My family'.

> TEACHER: Where's Daddy?
> GIRL: He's gone away.

There was news time.

> GIRL: My nan died last night.
> TEACHER: Oh dear. How sad. I expect she was very old.

And written news.

'My sister had a fit and she cube not brea (the) her eye went up.'

Changes in home circumstances, known semi-publicly, were commonly privately posed as having unfavourable consequences for the children's work and behaviour in school.

Felt left out and needed a lot of attention following birth of new baby.

Rather confused during period of mother's divorce.

The class project is Air. Malcolm has brought a large model aeroplane from home. He wants to take it out at playtime but teacher forbids it. She explains to me that he wants to attract attention. He should get enough at home as the only boy and youngest of three, but his father has been ill and he probably feels neglected.

Changes in home circumstances were not thought to have inevitable consequences in school, but when changes in school were not acceptably explicable in terms of development or illness in the child, the teacher actively sought knowledge of the home.

The teacher is concerned about Sharon who used to be well behaved but has recently become 'awkward'. Teacher, deliberately casual: 'Will Mummy and Daddy be coming to see me on Open Day, Sharon?' Sharon: 'I don't know, Mum's not been well.' Teacher, to me later: 'I knew there was something.'

As long as the home and school events occurred at roughly the same time they were assumed to be causally connected in the direction from home to school. This kind of explanation was posed even in the absence of any evidence.

Rather uncooperative lately. Trouble at home? (Teacher's end-of-year note)

Typification, responsibility, and innocence

To the teachers the process of typifying an individual child was one of building a picture of the way he or she was. They did not reflect on their own part in building the picture. Similarly, when changes in a child's work or behaviour were not acceptably explained in natural or developmental terms they were attributed to illness or home background, again leaving out the teacher herself as a possible factor. Two important consequences arise from their use of these explanations. Firstly, they were absolved from responsiblity for the undesirable changes; a child's bad behaviour or poor progress was not their fault. This protected their professional identity and left unquestioned their practices and the ideology they were based upon. Secondly, the child was also absolved from responsibility; bad behaviour or poor progress were due to factors beyond his control, he was innocent in intent.

The consequences of typification

Pictures or typifications constructed by the teacher were her definitions of what was 'real' about each child. The test of the 'reality' of social definitions used in the previous sections has been that based upon Thomas's proposition, 'they are real in their consequences'. Hence the question: What were the consequences of teachers typifying or defining individual children in particular ways? This is difficult to answer for a number of reasons. Each teacher typified each child in her class, and, as I have already described, I have accounts of only a few of these, and only indications of the hundreds of others from the teachers' verbal utterances in the classroom and their written accounts constrained by the format of record keeping. These typifications were not fixed, but, as I have described already, were modified over time. Furthermore, with the exception of the way teachers assessed and defined classroom behaviour, their typifications of the children were kept largely private. The definitions were real only to the teacher. This poses a further question: To whom were the consequences real?

Teachers' arrangements of their classrooms, the ways they dealt with children's writing, reading, number, and creative work, and the methods used to control their behaviour, were consequences of their definitions of the nature of children and the learning process, consonant with child-centred ideologies (Chapters 2–6). These definitions and the underlying ideologies were only real to the teachers. The consequences were real for both the teachers, in terms of their interactions with the children, and for the children who, as power subordinates in the interactions, tended to do and behave as their teacher arranged or allowed.

Similarly the teacher's definitions of individual children were only real for the teacher, but the consequences were real for both the teacher and the child. The teacher arranged for and allowed a child to do things in accord with her typification of the child. This was most obvious in the control of classroom behaviour.

> Mr Fish has 'one naughty boy'. 'Not bad really—every class has one. He can't sit still, he's always interfering with others.' His explanation: the boy's parents run a newsagent's, they are up early and close late, and have little time for him. He is left alone, unsupervised, and so has no self-control. 'A pleasant boy—quite like him really, but I have to keep on at him all the time.'

By the teachers' own reports children they typified as shy were 'drawn out', the nervous reassured, the 'easily upset' soothed, the uncertain given more attention, the boisterous were distracted, the solitary encouraged to mix. A child manifesting the typical properties of reading readiness was set to reading. (Chapter 3)

These consequences of typifications may suggest that the child was effectively what the teacher had defined him or her to be. But, as we have seen, the typifications were not fixed labels. They were modified in association with changes in the children who could be defined as 'spurting', 'calming down', or 'going through a naughty phase'. As the previous section showed, the teachers explained these changes in terms of development, illness or home background which excluded themselves as factors. Could these changes have been brought about by the actions of the teacher? This would imply that children were totally powerless and brought nothing into the classroom situation, made no contribution to their own learning and behaviour. In dealing with a particular child there is no acceptable way in which this proposition could be tested. We can only attempt to find the consequences in a given situation, and cannot know what they may have been had the teacher related to the child in a different way. (This point is returned to in Chapters 14 and 15)

None of this denies that in a given situation the teacher's typifications may have had real consequences for individual children. Children defined as ready to read were set to reading. However, this specific event in time cannot be regarded as determining who subsequently was defined as a poor or good reader. Even if an investigation showed that poor readers were those who were started later than good readers, a causal connection would not be established. Typification, assessment, teaching, learning, controlling, and being controlled were constantly modified in the flow of classroom interaction. Older children assessed and typified as good readers or 'over the hill' received less attention from the teacher than those defined as 'slow' readers, to be helped up the hill.

Individualism, typification, and conformity

In Chapter 1, I suggested that one of the main elements of the child-centred ideology was individualism, the recognition of the unique qualities of individual children. There was little individualism in what the children were manifestly taught or learnt. There was only one acceptable answer to a sum, and only one meaning to an arrangement of letters when reading or writing. When painting, drawing, doing craft work, projects, and 'free' writing, there was some scope for individual expression, but, as I have described in Chapters 3 and 4, this was constrained by the teachers' actions in accord with their ideologies of development and innocence, and the observance of conventional reality. Individual methods of learning were only used when that which was commonly used was judged by the teacher to be ineffective. This was most common when a child was 'stuck' in a particular reading scheme and was put on to another.

Individualism was mainly found in the typifications of individual children. It was through their 'pictures' of each child's unique developing personality that teachers felt they were dealing with the children 'as individuals'; it was in this way that 'they are all different'. Individual typifications were used to make particular explanations of the behaviour, progress, and peer-group relations of each child. These definitions had real consequences in the form of actions on the part of the teacher which attempted to bring about conformity. The 'shy' were 'brought out' and the 'boisterous' 'calmed down' in an attempt to bring both closer to the teacher's defintion of what a child should be. Thus an ironic consequence of defining children as individuals were attempts to reduce individuality.

Girls and boys

Teachers' public utterances were sometimes indices of their typifications of individual children. They also publicly differentiated between two groups of children—girls and boys. In every classroom boys hung their coats separately from the girls. They were lined up in separate rows at the door.

'Oh, Philip is a little girl. He's in the wrong queue.'

They were divided for activities.

> The class is acting Humpty Dumpty. Mrs Pink makes the girls horses and the boys king's men. Later on during music and movement, boys are houses and girls are rats.

Histograms of height or foot length were usually colour coded for sex. The bureaucracy was sex differential: the official record cards were colour coded, the registers listed boys and girls separately. These practices were completely taken for granted by the teachers, who, when I talked with them, generally said they had 'never thought about it', and that to divide the class by sex was 'convenient' and 'natural'. They were sometimes puzzled by what to them were my silly questions like, 'Why do you line the boys and girls up separately at the door?'

Sex differentiation was also used to promote competition among the children.

> 'Boys, don't sing. Listen to the girls, make certain they sing nicely. Now it's the boys' turn. Get your best singing voices ready. See if you can beat the girls.'

These practices indicated that teachers defined boys and girls as being different, that is, boys and girls, as kinds of pupil, were differently typified. David Hartley (1977), a doctoral research student, made a detailed study of sex differentiation at Burnley Road and the Langley school, following my own periods of observation. I mention his work to indicate that these brief comments hardly sketch the empirical and theoretical complexities of the sociological study of sex differences in education.

Teachers' public talk gave indications of how 'boys' and 'girls' were typified.

> A girl is trying to take a aeroplane jigsaw puzzle away from a boy. The teacher stops her, explaining, 'Boys like aeroplanes.'

Boys and girls were defined as having different interests, and this was confirmed for the teachers by their written and creative work. I carried out a content analysis of the 'stories' books of a class of rising sevens at Burnley Road. Every girl wrote stories and drew accompanying pictures with a domestic setting referring to home and children, and every girl wrote more of these stories than any other kind. Nine boys out of 14 wrote such stories, but all wrote more of other kinds of story, mostly concerning rockets, ships, planes, fighting, bombs, fires, crashes, and accidents. These were the occasional themes of only eight of the 13 girls.

In the practice of classroom control boys seemed to be named reprovingly more often than girls. (David Hartley has quantitatively confirmed this.) In the records there was a strong tendency for girls to receive more favourable assessments of behaviour. This was so for twelve out of fourteen teachers at Burnley Road, only one rated boys better than girls, and one rated them equally. At Seaton Park, eleven out of twelve rated girls the higher, and one rated boys so. At the Langley school fourteen showed more favour to girls, one reversed this, and one gave equal ratings. Boys were typified as being less well behaved than girls and this was regarded as being 'natural' and unremarkable.

Boys were also typified as making less progress in their work than girls. Slow readers received extra help from a part-time teacher at Burnley Road. Of the 56 referred to her only twelve were girls. She found nothing to explain in this. Neither did Mrs Baker of Seaton Park when I pointed out that of 29 children those reading progress she was checking because of their low reading ages, only six were girls. At Seaton Park only one teacher rated boys higher for attitude to work, in the school records, and at Langley only two did so.

If the teachers' definitions of boys and girls were real then they were real in their consequences. However, few consequences were obvious. At Burnley Road every teacher arranged for girls to hang their coats outside the classroom and the boys inside. They explained that 'you just can't trust the boys like you can the girls'. The paucity of obvious consequences has two explanations. Firstly, teachers related to their class as a group of children who were incidentally either boys or girls. Although the Plowden Report makes reference to sex differences they do not figure in the child-centred ideology. Some teachers explained that the boys were less mature than the girls, making sense through the developmental ideology. The taken-for-granted 'natural' sex differences were used to explain why some boys were poorly behaved or lacked progress.

This leads to the second point. In accord with their ideology teachers stressed the individuality of children and constructed typifications of individuals. These were more important than those they made of boys and girls as kinds of children. If their typifications of the sexes were the more important, it might be expected that they would rate all the boys in their class lower for behaviour and attitude to work than the girls. At the Langley school the teachers collectively rated 188 girls for conduct as follows: A 66.5, B 21.8, and C 11.7 per cent. The 227 boys were rated: A 35.7, B 41.9, and C 22.4 per cent. The percentages for attitude to work were for girls, A 61.2, B 30.9, C 8.0, and for boys, A 42.7, B 29.5, C 27.8.

In their everyday classroom world teachers seemed able to move easily from their definitions of the nature of all children to those of boys and girls in general, and to those of individual children who happened to be either boys or girls. All of these defintions may have had real consequences for the teachers and the children, but the problem is to know which was the more important in a given circumstance. Their definitions of children and the nature of learning seemed to have the broadest consequences for the curriculum, pedagogy, and forms of social control, and may therefore be considered paramount over those of individual children and certainly over those of boys and girls in general.

(Teachers also typified 'the children in this school' in ways described in Chapters 10, 12 and 13.)

CHAPTER EIGHT

Being the Infants' Teacher

I have described what I observed infants' teachers doing, and I have tried to explain why they did what they did in terms of their recipe ideologies of a child-centred education. Their definition of the classroom situation was consonant with their ideologies, as were their actions, which lead to it having 'real' consequences. Ideologies provide an over-arching conception of experience which is part of the way those who hold an ideology conceive themselves, that this, their social identities.

I have already outlined some of the problems in trying to explain the teachers' actions, but it is even more difficult to appreciate their experience of carrying out those actions. This is the distinction between doing and being. What is it like to be a teacher of infants? One way of answering this would have been to have become a teacher of infants. I did consider this possibility, but there were obvious practical drawbacks in terms of obtaining leave of absence from my university duties. More importantly, I would not have been an infants' teacher but a sociologist self-consciously doing, or trying to do, what he had seen teachers do. Doing is not the same as being. I have not received an infants' teacher's education; I would not have an infants' teacher's career. How would the other teachers, and more particularly the headteacher, relate to me, knowing, as they would have to know, that I was not an authentic colleague?

From this it follows that any treatment of the typical infants' teacher's identity will be rather limited, and I will draw principally upon teachers telling me about being a teacher. Secure in their ideologies, most teachers did not think a great deal about being a teacher, and so found talking about their experience even more strange than explaining why they did things. I will also describe the judgements that were made in the schools of the 'good teacher', and, in an effort to show what was particular about infants' teachers compared with other teachers, I will give an account of a small number of deviant teacher who were judged to be lacking some of the essential qualities of an infants' teacher.

The identity of infants' teachers

The characteristic manner of the teachers in their relationships with the children was marked by professional pleasantness, affection, and equanimity. They were aware of their use of this manner, and were willing to talk about it.

Professional pleasantness was part of being an infants' teacher. This was best seen when they were addressing a group of children, particularly on a public occasion, such as taking prayers, but it was in use in many classroom situations. Teachers talking to children had a special face, body posture, and a way of talking. They had bright, smiling faces, eyes stretched open wide, and used a great deal of eye contact. They walked with a bouncy movement. They stood up straight and still with feet together, often with arms folded or hands clasped in front of them, sometimes bending slightly at the waist, as the children were usually at a lower level. They spoke carefully and often slowly, using one of the several voices I have already described (Chapter 6).

The teachers were aware of being deliberately pleasant to the children. 'It's our job to keep them happy.' 'It's nice to be nice.' In calling this 'professional pleasantness' I am not implying it was either forced or false. It was part of being an infants' teacher. I saw only traces of it when they were being pleasant to one another, but it was often used when they talked to parents or when, initially, I was a stranger in the staff-room. I was congratulated on my new suit in just the same way as a boy with a new jumper. 'Oh, I say, I do like your new suit. Doesn't he look smart?' said with a big smile, in a bright voice, with just a slight, acceptably mocking edge to it.

After I recorded a teacher teaching I would play it back to her in order to discuss it. None had heard herself teach before. Although they knew they used a special voice with the children their initial reaction was always to the tone of their voice and speech delivery. They were amused or dismayed to hear how slowly they spoke and how much they sounded like Joyce Grenfell in her well-known sketch of an infants' teacher with her class.

Professional affection was an extension of their professional pleasantness. It was shown in their use of endearments, 'my love', 'dear', 'little one', 'sweetheart', and in their physical contact with the children, touching and patting their heads and shoulders, holding their hands, sitting them on their laps, and even occasionally kissing them.

This was professional affection in that they considered it part of being an infants' teacher. Those who were mothers themselves readily acknowledged that this affection was not the same as they felt or necessarily expressed in connection with their own children. Most teachers liked most of the children they taught but in many cases consciously controlled the amount of affection they allowed themselves to feel and express. This was because they knew the children would only be with them for a limited time, and they wished to avoid an emotional parting for themselves and the children. They also felt that too much affection might be bad for the children, it would 'keep them as babies'. Teachers who were the mothers of small children sometimes experienced conflict between their commitment to be pleasant, affectionate, and forbearing in school, and their exhausted capacity to be so at home. In one case it was 'my husband who gets all the snappiness'.

Professional equanimity was a remarkable feature. When the paints were split for the fourth time, when someone let the hampster out or wet his pants, the teacher usually showed little emotional response and stayed calm. Sometimes they marvelled at their own capacity for this professional equanimity. 'I don't know how I do it sometimes.' 'I often say to myself, keep calm and don't get upset.' When their equanimity was on occasion upset they sometimes felt guilty. 'I ask myself, now why did I have to do that?'

This conscious preservation of calm was related to the view that young children were innocent of bad intensions and could not be blamed. It was also a way of preventing emotional exhaustion. 'You can't afford to be upset all the time.' Some had found that being upset only upset the children. The mothers among them admitted that things that happened in the classroom were less important than the same things at home, and that they were usually more upset by incidents involving their own children than with those they taught.

The parallels between being the infants' teacher and being a mother were frequently stated by the teachers. 'We are their mothers while they're in school.' The more mature teachers whose own children were grown up spoke of the children they taught taking their place. When I pointed it out to some of them they agreed that being an infants' teacher was also rather like being a traditional housewife. They cooked, sewed, tidied, and even swept the floor. The image was completed by their putting on an apron to do these chores.

Classrooms were sometimes called the 'home base', and the teacher made it her own. Everything in it 'belonged' to her. Most tried to make their room a pleasant 'comfy' place. Their ownership was sometimes signalled by their introduction of carpets and furniture from their own homes. 'Homely' touches included putting curtains over open storage fitments, and flowers brought from their own gardens. They sometimes brought in the toys their own children had outgrown or discarded. This ownership was acknowledged by their colleagues who usually stood at the threshold waiting for a signal allowing them to enter. (The headteachers did not wait; it was their school.)

Although the dress of the teachers was quite varied, from arty–trendy to comfortable–conventional, there was usually an impression of a careful neatness in their appearance. In two of the schools the headmistresses constrained how the teachers dressed. At Burnley Road the principle was 'suitable dress for school'; this excluded trousers. The headmistress of the Langley school also banned trousers. This was the cause of some ill-feeling among the teachers, who complained to me that they often had to 'get down with the children' and so had blackened knees and ruined tights. Trousers, they thought, would be more practical and dignified garments. One day I was surprised to see most of them wearing trousers. They had made another appeal and to their evident delight the ban had been lifted.

Being an infants' teacher was not without its conflicts, strains and problems, but most teachers expressed considerable satisfaction with their job. They felt they were concerned with the most critical stage of education. They were generally content with the degree of autonomy they had in the classroom enabling them to have only the loosest kind of planning, to be able to 'play it by ear'. They obtained satisfaction in 'helping children to grow up'. Their efforts had visible outcomes: children who could not read or count at the beginning of the year could do so at the end.

The 'good' infants' teacher

In the early stages of my observations in each school the teachers maintained what David Hargreaves (1967) has called 'the myth of equal competence' about themselves. This was a form of colleague loyalty in the presence of a stranger, but when I became an insider it was clear that some were regarded as being better teachers than others. They signalled their judgements in their comments about one another, 'I expect you found it a lot quieter in Mrs Pink's', and in their conversations in the staff-room, 'Our Mary's a one and only'. Staff-room talk was mainly domestic: husbands, children, shopping, and about school affairs. The staff-room was used as a confessional when things had gone wrong. When Mrs Pink smacked Brian she told two other teachers on the way down the corridor to the staff-room, where she told everyone else over coffee (Chapter 6).

The headteachers did not support the myth of equal competence. They had well-established conceptions of the 'strengths and weaknesses' of each of their staff. They sometimes gave me an evaluative description or typification of the teacher I was observing or about to observe, which I tried to forget when making my observations. From these I was able to delineate the characteristics of the 'good' teacher. This was very similar for each head, although there were some significant differences.

The 'good' teacher's classroom was neither silent nor noisy; it had a 'busy hum'. The 'good' teacher's children behaved themselves in public places, such as the television-room and the hall, and made satisfactory progress with their learning. Her classroom was clean and tidy, although decked with the children's products. She completed her administrative tasks correctly: marking the register, collecting the dinner money, distributing notes for the children to take home. She came early in the morning and did not leave as soon as school finished. She came in before term started. She gave a good performance in taking assembly. The quality of her craft work was high. She showed professional pleasantness, affection, and equanimity; she had a 'very good manner' and 'likes her children'. Such paragons were rare, perhaps two in each of the schools, according to the headmistresses. Other teachers were measured against the model.

Mrs Brown at Burnley Road gave priority to the quiet hum and liked the classroom doors left open so that this was demonstrated. Having the door open was a sign of a 'good' teacher, and so some kept it open when it might have been better closed, as when they read a story above the hum of other classes using the corridor.

Miss Fox and Mrs Baker used forms of bureaucratic control over their teachers. At the Langley school they were required to produce a plan of work for each half term. At Seaton Park they had to complete a weekly report handed in each Monday morning. The headmistresses used these in their evaluations. From my observations there sometimes seemed only a slight resemblance between what happened in the classroom and what was either grandly planned or shortly reported. Many teachers acknowledged this, and regarded the plan or report mainly as a slightly bothersome written exercise to be completed in the required form and with correct spelling. When I asked about their actual planning many said they only knew what they were going to do on a given day just before it started. There were timetabled activities such as P.E., music and movement, and schools' television, but they kept enough flexibility for adventitious teaching, or for 'having a drive on the reading'.

How did the headmistresses make their assessments? They walked into classrooms, from time to time, to deliver messages. They also sent messages by the secretary or by a child but, as they told me, taking one themselves was a way of 'keeping an eye on things'. Once in the classroom they could see the children's work and behaviour, ask them questions or even take over the class for a while, sometimes to demonstrate to the teacher 'how it should be done'. They would glance into classrooms from outside, observe children around the school, catching a wanderer. 'Whose class are you in?' 'Does Mrs White know you are here?'

The teachers were well aware that they were being assessed by the heads, and at Burnley Road and Seaton Park their contributions to 'prayers' were viewed mainly in this way, and caused the anxieties already described in Chapter 5. Sometimes the assessment was made publicly. In Miss Fox's estimation Mrs Hart was over-affectionate towards her children. Teachers should 'like, even love' their children but not in a 'mushy' way (professional affection). Mrs Hart was doing neither herself nor her children any good; she was too emotionally involved and was keeping them too dependent upon her.

> There is a crush of children and teachers outside the hall. Mrs Hart picks up a small girl protectively. Miss Fox, in a public voice: 'Put her down, Mrs Hart, she's not a baby.' Mrs Hart looks shamed and flushed but holds on to the child for a short while longer before putting her down.

Later, in the staff-room, other teachers agreed with Miss Fox's implicit diagnosis, but not her treatment.

The evaluation of teachers by their colleagues used similar criteria to those of headteachers, and were made in similar circumstances, but also included looking after one another's classes, and taking children from a number of classes for hymn practice or watching television. Sometimes these colleague evaluations were quite public.

> Older teacher appears at doorway holding a coat and says to the younger one whose class it is, 'I don't want to tell tales but I found this on the floor in the corridor.'

Sometimes their approbation could be public. They denied there was any competition between them in the quality of their craft work for prayers. However, there was an anxiety about doing something original. When this was achieved the other teachers acknowledged it in the staff-room, and the recipient of this informal status would then share any of the technical know-how she had used, such as how to make translucent fish from grease-proof paper stuffed with pieces of crêpe paper and cooking foil.

Teachers were also evaluated by the secretaries, infants' helpers, caretakers and dinner ladies. Presumably they were evaluated by the children too, but I do not know how or on what criteria. Most of them had experienced only one or two teachers and would have little basis for comparison. Teacher was teacher.

Deviant teachers

The headteachers made evaluations of their teachers against their models of the 'good' infants' teacher. They usually explained teachers' shortcomings to me in terms of their lack of experience or their 'personalities'. But there were a few teachers of whom they spoke rather critically because they were regarded as not being 'proper' infants' teachers, a view shared by some of their colleagues. The explanation posed by the headteachers was that they were not infant trained. At first I thought this was just a claim for expertise based upon specialist qualifications, but on the first occasion of my observing one such teacher, I could see, having spent only a short time in her classroom, that she was not doing what other teachers typically did; she was not being an infants' teacher. In this sense and in the headteachers' definitions they were deviant teachers, and to some extent they were aware of it in referring rather defensively, even somewhat defiantly, to their lack of infant training, without my mentioning it.

The headmistress of one of these schools defined two such 'deviant' teachers on her staff; a man with a class of rising sevens and eights, and a woman with five- and six-year-olds. The woman, Mrs Panter, had an arts degree and had taken a secondary course for her postgraduate certificate in education, but the experience of teaching practice had led her to seek and obtain an infants' school post. The man, Mr Taylor, had been junior trained and had come from a junior school. His appointment, both as a man and as someone with junior school experience, was a consequence of the reorganization of the infants' schools in Newbridge to become first schools keeping the children until they were eight.

As a preliminary to the reorganization the local authority set up a working party discussion group consisting of a number of infants' school heads and teachers, and the adviser for primary education, with the teachers' centre warden (a part-time advisor) as chairman. The group first met in January 1970 and had fourteen meetings, the last in May 1971. All of these were observed either by Joan Fry or myself, or by my former colleague Gary Easthope. All three headteachers of the schools I studied were members, but none of their teachers were. The chairman and adviser were particularly keen to discuss the 'first school philosophy' and urged that reorganization was the opportunity for a radical reappraisal. The headteachers in the working party firmly rejected this. They saw the Plowden Report's recommendations of the setting up of first schools as an endorsement of the philosophy and methods of the present infants' schools. They therefore effectively div ted the meetings to deal mainly with the swapping of practical ideas (one was spent almost entirely on what could be done with plastic wine containers), and used the presence of the advisers to put their requests and complaints about supplies and finance to them directly.

The one thing that was generally agreed was that it might be desirable for the new first schools to have some men on the staff, and perhaps some teachers with experience of the lower junior age range. As a consequence some junior trained teachers, of which a few were men, were appointed to the newly created first schools of Newbridge, including Mr Taylor.

The headteacher's specific concerns about Mr Taylor were that he appeared not to like the children in his class, he kept them silent and only his voice could be heard. She had received complaints from parents about Mrs Panter's 'abrupt' treatment of their children: she was not concerned about Mrs Panter's ability to teach but with her manner and motives.

My observations of three teachers, defined by their headteachers as, in my terms, 'deviant', revealed the nature of their deviation. They showed little professional pleasantness, affection, or equanimity. They used mainly direct and not oblique control.

'Mark Williams don't you dare let me see you flick that paint.'

'I'm the boss, not you—tidy up.'

'Right then, stop it. I'm just about sick of you.'

Their typical style was one of impatient scolding and chivvying, using a do-as-I-say voice. They condemned bad behaviour more than they rewarded good, blaming the person more than the act, using shaming as a method of control.

'No, wrong. Do it again. Rub that out, it's all wrong.'

They did not generally define the children as innocent, and sometimes tried to force confessions of guilt.

Someone has shut the door against her expressed orders. She lines the five-year-old suspects up in the corner. 'Now you'll stand there until someone owns up. Somebody is telling fibs, and take that out of your mouth please. If you own up and say yes I won't be cross.' (She is cross now.) 'Will you take that sweet out Mark! Right, that's it, we're finished now.' The children stayed in the corner for half an hour but none confessed.

They publicly demonstrated their rejection of the model of the 'good' infants' teacher in their performance at 'prayers'. Although generally well prepared and competent they signalled, in Goffman's (1961) terms, considerable role-distance, effectively saying, in the headmistresses' and my interpretation, 'This is really a waste of time and I don't care much who knows it.' They were also effectively rejecting the child-centred ideology.

From the research point of view my discovery of these deviant teachers was most important in verifying the typical characteristics of infants' teachers as a professional class, and in confirming what I thought were their special qualities. If I were to single out one of these it would be that infants' teachers define the children they teach as being basically innocent in their intentions.

They were also important in illustrating the power of teachers, not only in controlling the activities of children but also in influencing their manifest disposition towards those activities. The head thought that the children in

Mr Taylor's class were less 'lively' and happy than they had been. My observations confirmed this, in that the children appeared more subdued and less eager than those in the five other equivalent classes. The teacher's definition of the situation not only had real consequences in the children's activities but also in their dispositions towards those activities. Mr Taylor complained to me, 'They've had all the play they need, now it's time to get down to some work.' They needed 'keeping down a bit'. He defined nothing as being 'exciting', 'interesting' or 'funny'; the children were not excited, interested or amused. Some teachers recognized the power of their definitions to have real consequences for the children. They, and I, could see that when they defined a sum as 'difficult' the response was often concerned faces; if it was 'easy', there were confident smiles.

Becoming an infants' teacher

I have mentioned the parallels between being the infants' teacher and being a mother and a housewife, parallels the teachers were well aware of. Can it be posed that being a teacher is an extension of being a woman? The two aberrant women teachers contradict this, as does the one male on the staff of Burnley Road. My observations in Mr Green's classroom showed him to work in a typically infants' teacher manner. The only conspicuous difference was his deliberate restraint in his physical contact with the children, for what he called 'obvious reasons'. When the children changed for swimming he always made sure one of the mothers was present. He did not feel that there was anything specifically feminine in being a teacher of young children.

Mr Green was infant/junior trained, and this was his first appointment. It seems reasonable to agree with his headmistress that courses specializing in infant education may produce a distinct kind of teacher. Colleges of education are the major institutions reproducing the child-centred ideology. Women (and some men) 'become' infants' teachers through their encounter with the ideology. This professional socialization theory might be modified by answering two questions about the selection process for such courses: what sorts of persons choose and are chosen to be educated for teaching young children?

CHAPTER NINE

The Three Schools and Their Catchment Areas

So far I have described activities I observed in the Burnley Road, Seaton Park, and Langley schools which represent what was similar about the schools, and I would expect to see similar activities in other infants' schools. Some were clearly seen in the much shorter periods of time spent in the 15 other infants' schools or departments in Newbridge when we were carrying out the general survey. The rest of the book is more concerned with the differences between the three schools, although some slight indications of these have been made already. Most of these will be differences in what I observed and differences in the teachers' definitions of the school and classroom situation. However, those described in this section were unknown to the teachers, at least in the form in which they are presented.

'Objective' 'facts' about the schools and the areas around them were obtained from three sources. Firstly, the 1971 Census figures for Newbridge. These were available at the enumeration district level of a few roads and a few hundred people. The education officers of Newbridge gave us details of the school catchment areas, so that it was possible to calculate certain social characteristics of these areas from the Census data. This was done for all 18 infants' schools or departments in Newbridge. Secondly, information was obtained from the general survey of these schools in 1972, gained through a questionnaire completed by the headteacher, interviews with the head and all the teachers, and short periods of observation. Following the reorganization of local government in 1973, Newbridge became part of the new county of Nossex. In 1975 the Nossex Social Services Department carried out a survey in Newbridge which forms a third source. The information was reported by ward divisions but fortunately the catchment areas of the three schools corresponded quite well with these, although some reservations about the figures should be made on this account.

I did not know most of this information whilst I was observing in the three schools. The calculations on the Census data, the analysis of the general survey, and the social services survey were all carried out afterwards. I chose to start observing at Burnley Road because it was a large school and because of indirect information about its social composition obtained from the headteachers of the local secondary schools concerning the occupations of the fathers of children in their first year and which primary schools they had come from. Since virtually all Burnley Road infants transferred to the adjacent junior school, this provided a rough social index of the former. I will describe the decisions to choose Seaton Park and Langley later (Chapters 12 and 13).

The Census data

The Census data concerning the catchment areas of the schools are, for a number of reasons, only rough social indicators of the schools themselves. There are the usual reservations to be made about the coverage, sampling, and methods used in such large-scale surveys. More importantly, none of the data available refers only to the children in the particular schools, indeed some of it does not refer to children at all. Some refer to adults who may include their parents, and to households which may include their own.

Table 1 Social class composition of school catchment areas (percentages)

	I Professional	II Managerial	IIIn Other non-manual	IIIm Skilled manual	IV Semi-skilled manual	V Unskilled manual
Langley	5.2	11.2	29.6	37.6	11.5	4.9
Seaton Park	2.8	6.6	31.1	44.3	7.6	7.6
Burnley Road	0.0	5.2	14.0	39.7	19.9	21.3
Newbridge	6.1	12.5	26.2	34.7	12.6	7.8

Source: Census 1971, Small Area Statistics 10 per cent sample.

Table 1 shows the social class composition of the school catchment areas and that for Newbridge as a whole. Most strikingly, the Burnley Road catchment area had the lowest proportions of professional, managerial, and other non-manual workers of any school in Newbridge, and the highest proportion of semi-skilled and unskilled manual workers. This was undoubtedly the most working-class area of Newbridge.

The catchment area of Seaton Park was mainly lower middle class and upper working class, having the highest proportion of social class III non-manual workers of any area, and the third highest proportion of or skilled manual workers. These two classes also predominated in the Langley area but the proportion of professional and managerial workers was higher, close to the Newbridge average, and that of unskilled manual workers the lowest of any area.

When children were brought to school for the first time their mothers completed an admissions slip which entailed filling in the father's occupation. These slips were kept in the children's files, and although not all were complete in this respect, they gave information about the social composition of the three schools. For Burnley Road the proportion of children whose fathers were non-manual workers was lower than that of adults in the catchment area, 13.0 compared with 19.2 per cent, as it was at Seaton Park, 36.9 compared with 40.5 per cent. However at Langley the reverse was the case. A higher proportion of children had fathers with non-manual occupations than the proportion found in the area; 51.2 compared with 46.0 per cent.

These differences may be due, in part, to the nature of the statistics themselves, but may also reflect another factor. Four parts of Newbridge were not in the catchment area of any school. Parents in these areas could choose to send their children to one of two or even three adjacent schools. These choice areas were mainly of new owner-occupied housing, but new schools had not been built as part of the developments. The populations were predominently middle class. Miss Fox proudly told me on several occasions how the Langley school received a number of children from such an area, and she attributed this to the 'good reputation' of the school. An inspection of the registers showed the existence of such children and the records showed them to be mainly middle class. These children may have lifted the social composition of the school into being marginally mainly middle class.

Although parents in a catchment area were supposed to send their children to the designated school, in an interview an education officer said that parents who objected and wished for a different school were often accommodated. I have no information about the incidence of these appeals or the nature of those appealing. However, both Mrs Baker at Seaton Park and Mrs Brown at Burnley Road told me that they 'lost' a number of parents this way and specified these as owner occupiers. Mrs Baker named the school these parents opted for, and when I interviewed the head there (before my time at Seaton Park) she told me proudly of the special transport arrangements these parents, from particular named roads, had made to send their children to 'her' school. It is possible that this element of parental choice may have increased the proportion of working-class children at Seaton Park and Burnley Road. This is therefore also a further caution in relating the school too closely to the statistics of the catchment area.

Table 2 Housing classes and conditions in school catchment areas (percentages)

	Owner-occupied	Council	Rented unfurnished	Rented furnished	All amenities (1)	Less than $\frac{1}{2}$ person per room
Langley	72.6	4.5	13.5	9.4	83.5	45.6
Seaton Park	38.8	58.0	3.0	0.2	98.5	22.4
Burnley Road	10.8	86.0	2.6	0.6	92.6	24.8
Newbridge	55.3	24.3	12.6	7.8	84.5	37.0

Note: (1) Hot water, bath, and inside w.c.
Source: Census 1971, Small Area Statistics. 100 per cent households.

Table 2 shows the housing classes and conditions in the catchment areas. The Burnley Road area had the highest proportion of council housing of any catchment area, and the lowest proportion of owner occupiers and rented accommodation. The school had in fact been built in 1931 at the same time as the 'slum-clearance' council estate surrounding it. The houses were well equipped with the basic amenities but were among the most crowded in the area, as were, in both these respects, those in the Seaton Park area. However, although these were mainly council houses over a third were owner-occupied. Owner occupiers predominated in the Langley area, one of the least crowded housing areas, with very few council houses.

Table 3 Social conditions in school catchment areas

	Children per married woman (1)	Lone parents (2) %	Unemployed (3) %	Persons with one car %	Persons with two or more cars%
Langley	1.4	11.0	3.4	52.9	9.0
Seaton Park	1.9	13.2	0.5	54.7	5.9
Burnley Road	2.6	19.3	7.2	36.6	4.3
Newbridge	1.6	10.2	2.9	49.6	10.2

Notes: (1) Children ever born to married women aged 16–39.
   (2) As proportion of all parents with dependent children.
   (3) Persons economically active but not in employment.
Source: Census 1971. Small Area Statistics. 100 per cent households and 100 per cent population.

Some of the general social conditions in the three areas are indicated in Table 3. Burnley Road had the highest number of children per married women (this includes the childless) of any area, as well as the highest proportion of lone parents and unemployed, but the lowest proportion of two-car owners. The Seaton Park area had the lowest level of unemployment in Newbridge but was about average on the other statistics except for two-car ownership which was low. The Langley area was close to average in these respects.

I should again stress that these figures do not relate directly to either the children in the schools or their parents. I was able to calculate the mean family size of the children in the schools from the records, and these were in the same order as the rather different measures quoted; Burnley Road, 3.6; Seaton Park, 2.8; Langley, 2.3. The proportions of children from incomplete families were calculated from the recorded parental separations, divorces, and deaths. This was 13.1 per cent at Seaton Park, close to the Census figure, and 26.2 per cent at

Table 4 Educational qualifications of populations in school catchment areas (percentages of persons in employment)

	Intermediate qualifications (1)	Higher-level qualifications (2)
Langley	8.8	5.2
Seaton Park	3.4	3.1
Burnley Road	0.8	0.3
Newbridge	7.7	6.0

Notes: (1) Includes A-level G.C.E., Higher School Certificate, O.N.D., O.N.C.
   (2) Includes H.N.C., H.N.D., nursing, teaching, senior professions, and vo-
      cational qualifications and degrees.
Source: Census, 1971, Small Area Statistics. 10 per cent sample.

Burnley Road, higher than the Census figure. Such records did not always take into account any subsequent reconciliation or remarriage. They were not kept at all in the Langley school.

Table 4 shows the paucity of adults with educational qualifications in the Burnley Road area, the lowest in Newbridge. The Seaton Park area was ranked sixteenth out of 18 for both levels of qualifications, but Langley was about average. Once again it is important to note that these qualifications were of all adults in the area not just those with children in the schools.

The social services survey

The report on the social services in Newbridge delineated the Burnley Road area as the 'problem area'. Table 5 shows it to have a large proportion of children 'referred' to the police in connection with theft, traffic offences, and other 'delinquent acts', and as being missing from home. The rate of social service referrals concerning families was the highest in Newbridge. These were made by general practitioners, health visitors, district nurses, hospitals, the education department, police, probation officers, the Department of Health and Social Security, parents, relatives, friends, and neighbours. The services included social work support, police liaison, home help, residential care, day care, psychiatric admission and after care, child-minders, adoption, fostering, school attendance, and housing. The general case load and that for family and children were the highest in Newbridge, two thirds of the cases in the special category concerned child neglect or moral danger.

Police referrals and case loads were about average in the Langley and Seaton Park areas, but family referrals were high around Seaton Park and low in the Langley area.

Table 5 Social services in school catchment areas: April–September 1974 (percentages)

	Police liaison referrals (1)	Social services case load (2)	Family and children case load (3)	Family referrals (4)
Langley	2.2	0.6	9.6	3.5
Seaton Park	3.4	0.6	7.5	11.0
Burnley Road	4.7	2.3	12.1	17.0
Newbridge	3.1	0.8	8.9	7.0

Notes:(1) As percentage of children 10–16.
     (2) For the total population.
     (3) As percentage of (2).
     (4) As percentage of social services referrals.
Source: Nossex County Council Social Services Department, 1975.

These statistics must be treated with caution as to their origin and collection. Some of them could not have related directly to children in the schools, and there is no way of knowing how many were referred to in the others.

The general survey of schools

The data reported from the Census and social services survey relate to conditions outside the schools. The general survey we conducted gathered data from inside the schools, but it too should be treated cautiously. The proportions of children receiving free meals shown in Table 6 may be seen to be in general accord with the statistics in previous tables.

Table 6 Some aspects of the schools

	Free dinners %	Material provision (1)	Pupil/teacher ratio	Teachers' experience in years (2)
Langley	6.8	2.5	35.0	7.0
Seaton Park	28.3	4.0	27.1	5.1
Burnley Road	37.5	3.5	28.3	2.5
All infants' schools and departments in Newbridge	16.6	2.2	28.6	3.3

Notes: (1) One point awarded for each of the following (range 0–4): dining area other than hall, swimming pool, games field on school site, indoor toilets. Half point for having only some indoor toilets.
(2) Mean of all teachers excluding headteacher.
Source: Survey of Newbridge primary schools 1972.

Burnley Road had the highest proportion of any school, Seaton Park was sixteenth of 18, whilst Langley had half the Newbridge average. The Plowden Report recommended the use of this statistic as a general index of the social composition of a school, and this is probably acceptable with respect to these three schools, although the conditions for receiving free meals have changed since the Report, and such factors as how many children went home to dinner and how many of those who were eligible did not apply for free meals are not taken into account.

The crude index of material provision shows a slight reversal of the expected trend with the Langley school scoring lowest, having no field on the school site. More detailed descriptions of the schools will be given later, but all were above average for provision among Newbridge schools. The high pupil–teacher ratio at the Langley school was a temporary state of affairs corrected by the time I made my observations. The significance of the differences in length of service of teachers, short at Burnley Road, longer at Langley, will be returned to later (Chapters 11 and 13).

The Plowden Committee invented the idea of the Educational Priority Area where schools with 'problems' were supposed to be most commonly found. The areas, and therefore the schools, were defined in demographic terms including the proportion of children receiving free meals, from large or incomplete families, defined as disturbed or handicapped, from overcrowded homes with low rateable values, and whose fathers have semi-skilled or unskilled manual jobs. On the basis of the data in the tables presented, it is clear that if any area of Newbridge were an E.P.A. then the Burnley Road area would be it. In 1975, after my main period of observations, Burnley Road school and its companion middle school were designated Social Priority Schools. This was the Nossex education authority's version of the E.P.A. school, and meant the teachers received an extra allowance, the capitation allowance was slightly increased, and the extra appointment of a 'compensatory' teacher.

I do not know if any of the demographic data I have reported here were taken into account in the designation of Burnley Road as an S.P.S. The headmistress, Mrs Brown, did not know either. She received a half-day visit from one of Her Majesty's Inspectors who, in asking her about the school, did not request any statistical information. Although by the time she told me this the school had been given S.P.S. status. I let Mrs Brown have some of the data reported here for her school and Newbridge in general.

'Knowing' the schools

Given all the reservations I have made about the data presented it may reasonably be asked why they were presented at all. I did so for the following related reasons. Despite the reservations the data have a useful 'objectivity' in that they were not created by the teachers, or, other than through secondary calculations, by me, except for the general survey of the schools which was my design and was carried out under my direction. This 'objectivity' of some of the data can be set against my observations in which I tried to be as objective as possible. It can also be set against the teachers' subjective definitions of the catchment area and the children in each of the schools; their knowing was often close to the statistical 'facts' which they did not know.

CHAPTER TEN

Social Priority School, Burnley Road—
The Definition of the Situation

'We are the E.P.A. school of Newbridge.' Mrs Brown made this claim the first time I went to Burnley Road to ask her for help with my research. I have already described how subsequently this was fulfilled by the school being officially designated S.P.S.

Burnley Road infants' school was opened in 1931, in the words of His Majesty's Inspectors' report of 1936, 'to meet the needs of a new housing area associated with a slum clearance scheme'. The 1971 Census data, already reported, echoes the social conditions implicit 40 years before. The catchment area was the most working class in Newbridge, with the highest proportion of unemployed and of council house tenants. The average family size was the highest of any catchment area, as was the proportion of one-parent families. The social services officially defined it as the 'problem area' of Newbridge.

Most of these 'facts' were not apparent when walking or driving during the day in the Burnley Road area. The immediate impression was of rows of uniform red-brick terraced houses behind small front gardens, whose lack of variation in paintwork and fittings, such as doors and gates, signalled their council house status. Among the neat and tidy front gardens were others untended and a few with the appearance of dumps. It was common to see small children playing on the pavements in streets, which apart from the main road outside the school itself, were fairly free from traffic. The area had its own shops and pubs built at the same time as the school, but no factories or other places of large employment other than shops and garages.

The school was a single-storey brick building with most of the classrooms arranged around an L-shaped corridor. There was an outdoor swimming pool and a grassy playing area shared with the adjacent junior (later middle) school. Architecturally the school and the surrounding houses were in accord: pleasant, 1930s municipal–functional.

The teachers would have seen all this and more as they drove to school each day, either in their own cars or to be dropped off by their husbands. But their major encounter was with the children they taught, and this account is concerned mainly with the way the teachers defined the children of Burnley Road, and with the consequences of their making this definition. These processes involved elements clearly related to the data of the surveys referred to, although the teachers were unaware of their existence. Parts of what follows were discussed with individual teachers during the follow-up to particular observations in their classrooms. The whole of the following exposition was first made in essentially the same form at a meeting of all the teachers in which they broadly endorsed it as their 'way of seeing things', and generally concurred with the explanations I posed about it. This is my interpretation of their shared definitions of the children of Burnley Road and the consequences of the 'reality' of this definition, and my explanation of the processes involved.

Defining the children

Individual teachers typified or defined each of the children in their class. They also typified 'the children in my class' and, by extension, 'the children in this school'. In talking among themselves or to me they would move easily from the individual to the group definitions. The typification of the 'children in this school' was related to and partly constructed from those of the individual children, although it was more than just the collectivity of them. Thus there was no apparent problem for teachers when the definition of an individual was at variance with that of the group. (If I typify 'my students' as hardworking this does not contradict my occasionally typifying one as lazy.) Furthermore, whereas the typifications of individual children were made by individual teachers and kept largely to themselves, that of 'children in this school' was shared among all the teachers.

The shared nature of the definition was only properly confirmed at the end of the year's observations, but its nature became reasonably clear after a few weeks. The teachers were initially reserved in talking about the children to any strangers, but once I was accepted, in the words of the headmistress, Mrs Brown, as 'one of the family', they did talk, on the basis of 'you've seen what they [the children] are like'; implying that their definition was apparent to any insider to the school.

In typifying individual children teachers assessed their learning progress, their compliance with classroom rules, and their relations with other children. The first two elements were part of the typification of 'children in this school' held by individual teachers and shared by all. Children at Burnley Road school were defined as making less than the expected progress in their learning, and as not being readily compliant with classroom rules, especially the boys. In the words of the teachers themselves they were 'below average', 'not too bright', 'a bit slow', 'need a lot of help'. In the classroom they were 'very lively', 'quite a handful', 'not house-trained', and 'you can't afford to take your eyes off them'. I should stress that holding these definitions of the collectivity of children did not prevent teachers defining individual children as 'bright' (although 'we have no really bright ones to give the others a lead') and 'nicely behaved'.

How did this collective definition come to be made? In typifying individual children teachers drew mainly upon their immediate experience of the children in the classroom, and this too was the basis of their typification of children in the school. Children's progress in the three R's was continuously assessed. In reading it was marked by the book they were on. The teachers' definition of slow progress was confirmed by calculations from the school records. On average the children in the school were 2.1 books below what the author of the Ladybird Series considered average for their age. Since each book represents six months the children were over 1 year 'behind'. The discrepancy was bigger for boys (2.5 books or 1.25 years behind) than girls (1.6 books or over nine months behind). After my year's observations the new Nossex local authority obliged all the rising sevens in the area to take the Young Group Reading Test. The mean reading quotient was 82.2 (boys 78.5, girls 86.9).

A set scheme for mathematics, such as the Fletcher books, was not used at Burnley Road, so that it is not possible to independently confirm the teachers' definition of slow progress in maths and number. Progress in reading and writing were closely allied, and teachers commonly pointed out the repetitious nature of the children's writing, sometimes to the children themselves.

> 'We're not having someone going to hospital again please. We've had someone going to hospital for at least five days. Think of something else please.'

Their drawings and paintings, too, were sometimes considered limited in range of content.

The teachers related two other characteristics to the children's level of progress in learning: their speech and their knowledge of things. Most of the children spoke with a local accent but this was not the teachers' main concern, although some mispronunciations were corrected. Their concern was with the children's 'ability to express themselves'. In practice this was answering teacher's questions. (They were also concerned that the children asked so few questions.) Some teachers felt that children knew more than they could express. In other contexts, including the playground and when talking to one another in the classroom, the children were far from verbally inexpressive. However, in the teachers' terms some were virtually 'silent'.

Burnley Road was the only infants' school in Newbridge to have regular visits, twice weekly, from the speech therapist. When I interviewed her she had currently 29 regular 'patients', the highest incidence of any infants' school in the area. She defined some as pathogenic, with palate, tongue or brain disorders, such as aphasia. However '75 per cent' were non-pathogenic, 'silent' or 'wordless' children, characteristic of the school, and she had set about persuading the teachers to refer such pupils to her. The Peabody or Matrix Test showed that these children had 300–400-word vocabularies instead of the 2000–3000 words 'they should have'.

Lack of verbal ability was thought to limit the children's capacity to express what they knew, but the amount of their general knowledge was also judged to be limited. Some children came to school apparently unable to recognize colours. I observed one class where not one 5-year-old identified, verbally or by pointing, the colour pink when asked by the teacher. Among 6-year-olds several seemed unable to say their addresses when asked. Few children seemed to know their birthdays when asked. None of a class of 5-year-olds appeared to have heard of

Jesus. Sometimes they appeared unable to recognize things that the teacher thought they should be familiar with.

> Someone has brought in a pine cone. Teacher holds it up. 'What's this?' 'A conker.' 'Acorn.' 'Shell thing.' She has to tell them.

In 'discussions' teachers frequently found themselves reluctantly telling children things they (the teachers) thought they ought to know already.

> The class have just watched a television programme on canals.

TEACHER:	What is the difference between a canal and a river?
FIRST PUPIL:	Both the same.
SECOND:	Canals are like little things.
THIRD:	Canals are thinner.
FOURTH:	Canal got a gate.
TEACHER:	Who makes a river?
FIFTH PUPIL:	Rain.
TEACHER:	Very clever. If you have something to say put your hand up. Not now, I'm speaking. Rivers are made by rain. What about a canal?
PUPIL:	The sea's a canal.
ANOTHER:	Canal's got electric wires under it.
TEACHER:	I'll have to tell you. A canal has been made by people. It is usually straight. Some rivers are straightened, but usually they curve.

This kind of exchange is also an example of what the teachers called the children's 'lack of concentration'. They had not 'concentrated' on the programme (they were quiet and appeared attentive as I observed them) and had not 'concentrated' on the way she tried to lead them to an acceptable answer. 'I find myself repeating things all the time.'

In the end-of-year assessments of 'conduct' for the official record card, 57.7 per cent of children received a positive evaluation from their teacher, 23.2 per cent a neutral or mixed one, and a minority of 19.1 per cent a negative evaluation. This distribution, on the teachers' own admission, concealed more than it revealed about how they 'really' defined the children's behaviour. Their less favourable definition was based upon day-to-day occurrences which I observed and which individual teachers referred to. ('You've seen what they are like.')

Most of the classrooms, much of the time, were as quiet and orderly as any I observed in other schools, but in all classrooms both the teacher and I could see from time to time some children, covertly or openly, pinch, push, punch, bite, scratch, kick, spit, and shout at other children. Sitting down on the floor for story time, lining up at the door, and doing music and movement were sometimes the occasions for minor scuffles. Other children's careful constructions were sometimes deliberately knocked over, their writing scribbled on, their paintings splattered, the toys they were playing with snatched away. At milk time there could be milk flicking, blowing bubbles through the straw, making noises sucking up the last drops. Keeping the classroom tidy was a constant 'problem' for the teachers. From time to time toys, pencils, and other things 'went missing'. One boy stole money from three teachers' handbags including the headmistress's.

The occasional incidence of this kind of behaviour does not mean that every classroom was always noisy with squabbling children. The general impression that most visitors had of the children was of lively cheerfulness. They could be quiet, busy, and show kindness and cooperation.

Like me, the teachers observed the children's behaviour, but they also judged it. Their judgements were made on a number of bases. Those of work progress rested on the authority of the author of the reading book and the reading tests of psychologists. But they also drew upon their own previous experience in judging the children's progress and behaviour. Those who were mothers compared them unfavourably to their own children (but not always; one thought she had one boy as 'bright' as her own son at the same age). They reflected on their own education. 'They never told us children could be like this at college', and even on their own childhood, 'I never behaved like that when I was their age'. They compared Burnley Road to other schools they had taught in.

Mr Green did his teaching practice in 'the posh suburbs', the 'stockbroker belt' of Manchester, where many children could read before they came to school and knew the rules of number. 'I'd just go in and write the date on the board, the children would arrive and get on with their work. I felt redundant. Here you have to make decisions all the time and work all the time. They bring nothing useful in the way of experience.'

Where teachers typified individual children they kept most of the typifications private, but the definition of 'children in this school' was shared among the teachers, and the sharing process took place mainly in the staff-room conversations. Here such incidents as the stealing of calendars, running out of the playground, kickings, and smackings (by teachers) were reported to colleagues, who would sympathize, recall similar incidents that had happened to them, and sometimes pursue wryly humorous fantasies about what they would like to do about it.

Much of the talk centres around an incident involving a boy who was in a 'temper' the previous afternoon. He wanted to go home. The teacher removed his shoes. 'Not because he was kicking me—I'd kick him back.' The others join in. 'We need a padded cell in this place.' 'Soundproof too.'

These comments were not meant seriously, they were never malicious and always private from the children. On other occasions children were spoken of kindly and even affectionately. I saw at least as much professional equanimity, pleasantness, and affection on the part of Burnley Road teachers as any others.

The definition of 'children at this school' was made real through day-to-day occurrences which the teachers knew their colleagues also experienced. In talking to the teachers about this I used a dream analogy. How do we define a dream as a dream and not 'real'? We have different dreams each night and we alone dream them. (We assign special significance to a dream that is repeated.) The reality of everyday life is grounded on repeated experiences shared by others.

The family–home background theory

Ideologies are both empirical and evaluative; they not only express what is thought to be but also what ought to be. The child-centred recipe ideologies of infants' teachers defined children as they ought to be and the teachers acted in such a way as to try to make children be as they ought to be; to fuse the 'ought' with the 'is'. Unfavourable changes in the progress or behaviour of individual children that could not be defined as 'natural' by the teacher were explained in terms of the child's health or home background (Chapter 8). At Burnley Road the progress and behaviour of children in general were unfavourably judged by the teachers individually and collectively. There was a gap or discrepancy between the 'ought' and the 'is'; the children were not as children should be. In the teachers' terms they had few 'ordinary' or 'normal' children.

As when typifying individual children they explained this discrepancy in terms of the children's health and home backgrounds, basically a family–home background theory. At its most simple their poor behaviour and progress were due to the conditions and the way they were brought up. The teachers collectively defined the typical family as large, with a low income. The parents were 'not very bright', sometimes in 'trouble' with the police and other officials, and some had histories of chronic physical and mental illness. The fathers were often 'out of work' or 'in and out of work', drank too much, and could sometimes be aggressive. Their wives were not good at household management and were poor mothers, sometimes neglecting their children's nutritional state, health, and clothing, providing little to stimulate their minds and widen their experience. Some children were from broken homes where 'boy-friends' had taken the place of the husband.

It is important to note that this typification of 'the sort of homes our children come from' was held with others of the homes of individual children which were defined as 'pleasant, ordinary people', 'a good, caring home', 'a really good mother'. As with apparently contradictory typifications of individual children with 'children in this school', teachers talked of such individual homes and 'the sort of homes our children come from' with no sense of contradiction.

How was this typification constructed? The teachers drew on their experience and observations of both the children and their parents. Many, perhaps most of the children were as clean and as well dressed as any I saw elsewhere, but in every class some were conspicuously dirty. Changing for P.E. or swimming revealed black ankles. There were grimed knees, elbows, necks, and ears, black finger nails, dried food on faces, and yellowed teeth. Watching television on one occasion a small girl insisted on sitting on my lap. I discovered why the teachers often refused this when asked; her smell of stale urine remained with me for the rest of the day. Each classroom had an aerosol air freshener supplied from stock to 'clear the air' when required. One teacher told me that some of her colleagues actually sprayed the children, but I never saw this, and I suspect it to be apocryphal, but revealing. Congealed nasal mucus was not uncommon.

TEACHER: Have you got a handkerchief?
BOY: No.
TEACHER: Come and get one. [A paper handkerchief on her table. He goes to pick the mucus off.]
TEACHER: Don't do that!

Some children wore plastic shoes, shoes too big for them, or too small with backs splitting, socks with holes in, matted, dirty, woollen wear with frayed sleeves and the elbows out. About a quarter of the children had no plimsolls for P.E. The teachers said that their parents were only prepared to buy them one pair and then no more. Some boys wore no pants, one had a pair of girl's knickers for swimming, which did not go unnoticed by the other children. In the winter the topcoats of some children were old and dirty, too big or too small, with broken zips and missing toggles.

Some children had dirty, unhealed sores on their hands or legs. Others had cuts and bruises on their bodies which they could or would not explain to the teachers, who felt they were too frightened to do so, and suspected the parents. A few children looked tired all day long. Some were officially medical cases, including one case of worms, and the teachers were responsible for giving them their medicine. One boy had started school who was not toilet trained and was taken into hospital for a fortnight to accomplish this. Toilets were often left unflushed, a job that the teachers, according to Mrs Brown, the headmistress, felt was 'beneath them', so she made it her job to do it.

The toys and books that children brought to school from home were often not approved by the teachers, although they did not show this directly. Guns and tanks and other toys were kept in her drawer 'to keep them safe' and to prevent their being lost or stolen or giving rise to disruptive play. Disapproved annuals, often conspicuously second-hand even when recently received as a present, were politely admired but not read. When a trip was arranged to the Newbridge museum the teacher discovered that it was the first time that some of the class of 6-year-olds had been into 'town', 2 miles away.

The teachers' direct encounters with the parents, principally the mothers, were when they brought and collected the younger children either from the playground or classroom, and on special occasions such as Open Day or the Christmas Concert, after which I made the following notes:

> Mothers wear cheap, sometimes dated, old and sometimes dirty clothes. Not casual clothing but 'dressed up' clothes. High heels, fancy boots, fur-collar coats. Some are heavily made up with unwashed hair.
>
> The adults and children of the audience are very noisy particularly when the performing children are talking. Some of the teachers show facial disapproval. (Mrs Brown says, 'They get furious.') One says, 'Shss.' Is it to the children, the parents or both? It doesn't work.
>
> Audience invited to join in 'Once in royal David's city'. They do not.
>
> Mrs Brown gives an address to the parents at the end of the performance. The noise continues. 'I expect our children enjoyed it more than you did because you were not able to hear the words.' There seems no audience reaction—is it meant for the teachers? She ends by saying, 'You can see why at Burnley Road it is necessary to train all these little ones to be quiet.' They laugh! I'm not sure it was meant as a joke. There was a kind of tight-lipped smile.

The basis of the teachers' hostility on this occasion was that they and the children had worked hard for months preparing the gorgeous costumes and rehearsing their pieces, and their own parents could not keep quiet to hear them perform.

However, in encounters with just one parent the teachers were always pleasant and smiling, as on Open Day when, they admitted later, they deliberately put on their smartest appearance to stress the difference between themselves and the mothers. They all had tights on although the day was hot and the day before most had not worn them. On this occasion many mothers had babies with them, and there were toddlers wandering all over the school, sometimes pursued by shouting women. On the basis of the previous year's experience Mrs Brown rigorously excluded all dogs.

The record files contained some notes about the parents, but when I commented on them Mrs Brown said they were incomplete because 'we keep that kind of thing in our heads'. To prove this she took an exercise book and went round to each classroom asking the teacher to tell her about any 'problems' concerning the children in their class. They made notes on just over half (50.1 per cent) of children in the school. The 391 comments included the following:

Unhappy home—mother badly treated.

Lives with father and grandmother—mother has left them.

Father knocks mother about.

Continual turnover of 'uncles'. Mother in violent fights in street.

Mother convicted of 'baby bashing', has been in care.

Very poor home, large family, unable to cope.

Problems in the family. Going to child guidance clinic.

Parents separated. Mother has what children call 'fancyman'.

The following list gives the frequency of types of comments for all children in the book. (The frequency in the school population would be roughly half.)

	%
Irregular family ('boy friends', uncles')	19.4
Parents separated or divorced	19.4
Large family	18.0
Family experience of courts or prison	14.8
Parents 'inadequate'	14.4
Pathological experience in family	11.8
Absent father	9.8
'Bad' home conditions	6.2
Speech problems	5.6
Parent(s) 'unstable'	5.2
Violent fathers	4.8
Father unemployed or 'never in work'	4.6
Parents 'uncooperative'	4.6
Illigitimate	4.6
Child 'dirty'	4.6
Evidence of home conflict	3.6

Absent mother	3.6
Truancy and/or poor attendance	3.6
Child 'ill-treated'	2.6
Parents 'dim but cooperative'	2.0
Child in chronic ill-health	2.0
Child fostered	1.6
Child guidance clinic visited	1.6
Child 'immature'	1.6
Child 'neglected'	1.6
Parents 'a bad influence'	1.6

Where did the teachers get this 'knowledge'? Firstly, from the children themselves, in their writing, drawings, and talk at news time. Sometimes they could see a mother relating to her child.

> Mother gives her son a kiss before leaving him in the classroom. 'Remember be a good boy or I'll get my stick.' Boy: 'I'll break your stick.' Mother: 'My stick'll break you!'

Individual teachers had been frightened by aggressive parents, particularly fathers, on the rare occasions when they had been seen. Mrs Brown had been physically attacked twice. One father had broken into her office in the evening, forced open a filing cabinet, and stolen the dinner money. The stockroom door, left open all day, was locked after school, following thefts by 'light-fingered parents'. The social agencies let Mrs Brown know when they were involved with children or their families and she passed this on to the class teacher, who was sometimes charged to keep an eye on the child in question. In one case a boy had a small rupture sustained, it was suspected, by being 'interfered with' by his mother's boy-friend. Teachers read about some of the parents' court appearances in the local paper.

Burnley Road was the only infants' school in Newbridge to have a regular weekly call from the educational welfare officer, and he added to the stock of knowledge. He told of his encounter with the drunken lover of an alcoholic mother of one of the children, who had been found wandering alone late at night. 'Have you come to snog with her?'

The prospect of visiting the children's homes frightened some teachers, but they did so in special circumstances.

> Someone found a 4-year-old in the boys' toilets wearing a plastic crash helmet with his first name on and carrying a box of cornflakes. The local shop knew his address and Mrs Black took him home. After several attempts at knocking the mother came to the door and said he had been sent to his aunt's and she didn't want him. Later it was discovered that the boy has a sister at the school but she has a different surname. Mrs Black described the mother as a young slut with hair in curlers, cigarette in her mouth, wearing fur slippers.

All this was recounted in the staff-room where the knowledge of children and their parents was shared among the teachers. There was sometimes a rather prurient tone to their discussions of the 'irregular' family arrangements they heard about, and they sometimes become indignant on behalf of the children who experienced a succession of 'uncles' or had fathers convicted of incestuous relations with their older sisters. I should stress that their judgements of parents were never made to the children themselves, and that not all parents were so judged. Sometimes the teachers could be affectionately mocking about parents in the staff-room, joking about the misspelt notes they sent, explaining that their child had been 'bad all night', or that they had been 'under the doctor for a fortnight'.

Unknown to the teachers the school log-book showed that their definitions of the children and their home backgrounds had been made throughout the history of the school. The H.M.I.'s report of 1936 referred to 'the slower children of which there appear to be a good number'. In 1950 the H.M.I. wrote, 'The nature of the area served by this School makes special demands upon the headmistress and her staff.' In 1958 the H.M.I.'s report referred to 'the high incidence of less able children', and to 'the crowded unstable conditions under which the children live'.

The teachers did not know the Census or social services survey for the area, but they did 'know' in their own way what those data referred to.

Why this 'theory'?

Why did the teachers pose the theory that the children's poor progress and behaviour were due to their home backgrounds? Firstly, they were not alone in posing the theory. It was confirmed by experts, including the educational psychologist, to whom, according to the school records, 20 children had been referred. This was a typical report:

WISC Verbal Scale   IQ 85   Perf. IQ 84   Full scale IQ 84
   Mark is a confiding and friendly little boy, rather small for his age and the bearing of a socially deprived child.
   The results of the Wechsler test show that he has low average intelligence, though I suspect that he is underfunctioning because of his home background and the general circumstances of his life. The little boy scored lowest on a test of general information and a poor score on this item always indicates an inadequate family background.
   Mark's slow reading appears to be due to the following circumstances:
   (1) An impoverished and unstimulating home background. Mark seems to be fourth of six children in a family which falls in the lower socio-economic group.
   (2) Lack of stimulation and motivation to succeed.

This kind of report endorsed the theory (although I never heard a teacher use the phrase 'socially deprived'), and confirmed with expert authority what the teacher already 'knew'.

The speech therapist made public her view of 'wordless homes with wordless mothers and wordless children'. The eventual designation of being a Social Priority School further endorsed the 'theory'.

More importantly, the family–home background 'theory' preserved two important ideological elements for the teachers. Firstly, the innocence of the children. They could not be blamed for their lack of progress or poor behaviour, which were due to their backgrounds.

'It's all due to the family. I know they're annoying but they aren't really responsible.'

A few teachers were reluctant even to blame some of the parents, and expressed sympathy for the plight of young mothers of large families struggling to bring them up on very little money, and posed, in a vague way, that the general social order was to blame.

Secondly, the 'theory' meant that the children's lack of progress and poor behaviour were not the fault of the teachers, which meant that their methods and practices were not questioned nor were the child-centred ideologies underlying them. The sharing of the definition of the children and of the 'theory' was important in reassuring the individual teacher that she was not failing, that what happened in her classroom was happening in all the others in the school.

Institutionalized ideologies create order and meaning for people's lives in realizing their identities. The difference between what the teachers' child-centred ideologies defined a child ought to be and what their experience showed the children of Burnley Road 'actually' to be, put a strain on the ideology and upon their identities as good infants' teachers, engaged in the most important and critical period of a child's education. The family 'theory' relieved this strain preserving the ideology and their professional identities which would otherwise have been questioned.

What I have presented here is my theory of the teachers' 'theory', my understanding of their understanding, both of which they endorsed.

CHAPTER ELEVEN

Burnley Road—The Consequences of the Definition

The consequences of defining the 'children in this school' as slow in their progress and poor in their behaviour were seen in the organization of the school and in the actions of the teachers in the classrooms. There were also consequences seen in Mrs Brown's actions and policies as headteacher, but these were also related to the definition of the parents and to the family–home background theory.

The adjustment class

The adjustment class was an organizational element found only at Burnely Road among the infants' schools and departments of Newbridge. It and its name had existed before Mrs Brown's headship. Mrs Black had been the class teacher for a number of years. She had 14 children—ten boys and four girls. Some had been in the class since arrival at the school, if medical, child care or health visitor reports suggested they should. Others were transferred from other classes either because of their slow progress or because the teacher 'couldn't cope with them'. Some stayed for the whole of their school career, others for a year, which 'does the trick', and were returned to other classes; they were 'adjusted'. Mrs Black explained the sex ratio by saying, '90 per cent of the trouble in this school is due to boys.' The girls were in her class because they were 'slow', the boys because they were 'slow' and/or troublesome.

Mrs Black claimed the children felt no stigma about being in the class, which was always referred to as 'Mrs Black's class' or 'Class 14' (the room number). I found no evidence to contradict this or to suggest that other children in the school gave it special status. According to Mrs Black it was the parents of the children in the class who called it the 'daft class'.

Some of the children did not proceed to the junior school but to the school for the educationally subnormal. This was on Mrs Black's recommendation, endorsed by the headteacher, the educational psychologist, and the medical officer, but with the final approval of the mother. After one had categorically turned down the offer for the 'daft school', Mrs Black began to take the mothers down to the E.S.N. school in her car, to introduce them to the headteacher and show them around. She said they were impressed, and agreed with her that going there was in their child's best interests. One mother who had two children there already 'thinks she's putting their names down for Eton'.

Mrs Black's colleagues held her in some respect, and her class in some apprehension. If she were called out of her room both infants' helpers were called in to take her place for a few minutes. When she was away her children were dispersed in twos or threes to other classes. 'They couldn't cope with any more.'

Inside Class 14 was Burnley Road writ large. The children were almost all poorly dressed and dirty. The door was kept permanently closed, against the school norm, to prevent the children 'escaping'. None of the children was 'up to' doing his own writing, and mainly copied or traced over things written by Mrs Black. No child was above Ladybird Book 2 (reading age 5). A few were quiet, almost silent, but most were noisy, talking, singing, making burps and raspberries. occasionally shouting words or phrases, some of them obscene, but with every appearance of being generally happy, although some looked tired even at the start of the day. Some worked or played quietly together but others threw and fought over toys, kicking, punching, and spitting.

Mrs Black was the epitome of professional equanimity. She used little public voice, moving around the classroom all the time, settling quarrels, tidying up, preventing accidents, talking to the children, and showing them how to do things. She physically moved the children very skilfully, almost casually in passing, as a routine, not as an exception as in other classes. When someone cried or made a direct appeal to her over a dispute she laid no blame, her general reaction being, 'Well that's what happens when you throw things or when you're being silly.' She felt that some of the children tried to see 'how far they could go' with her. Two boys sat under the table at story time. She asked them to come out several times. Finally she dragged them out looking a little cross but determined. The boys looked as if they expected it to happen.

Despite the noise and disruption Mrs Black felt she was in control. When she left the class in the charge of the two infants' helpers there was 'chaos' but as soon as she looked through the window on her return they quietened down. When she had been away they were pleased to see her back and anxious about her going away again. She counted her successes in terms of those returned to other classes, and saw some 'progress' in those who stayed with her longer.

Mrs Black's definition or typification of the children in her class was similar to that of other teachers but with a special element. Basically their poor attainment and behaviour were attributed to their parents and home background. Most of the children were from large families (ten from families of more than five children) and tended to be the youngest. Mrs Black spoke of poor, exhausted mothers having to go out to work so that the last-born was most neglected. Some of the parents were described as E.S.N. since it was 'known' that they had been pupils at the E.S.N. school. Some children had physical handicaps which Mrs Black regarded as an extra 'burden' and not the basic cause of their 'problems'. These included epilepsy, mild deafness, and palate troubles, all medically certified.

Extra reading

The definition of poor reading progress was accepted by the local authority enabling Mrs Brown to appoint Mrs Gray on a part-time basis. Mrs Gray had 56 children regularly referred to her by class teachers because they 'need extra help with their reading'. They came from the top classes only and were no higher than Ladybird Book 2. Mrs Gray aimed to get them to Book 6 or 7 by the end of the year. 'They *should* be up to 7.' She felt satisfaction with the 'progress' that most made, although a few made little. She was anxious that they should not be stigmatized in being sent to her so she arranged for a few 'good' readers to go to her as well. This was done clandestinely since Mrs Brown did not approve.

In Chapter 3, I mentioned the book club at Burnley Road which met two or three times a term. This, too, was an attempt to help the children's reading, and about half of each class participated in the special savings scheme.

The consequences in the classroom

The 'children in this school' were defined as being poor in progress and behaviour but the family–home background theory preserved them from responsibility for these properties. However, absolving the children from blame in this way did not prevent the teachers defining their progress and behaviour as 'problems'. Coping with these problems without blaming the children and preserving their child-centred ideology constituted a set of dilemmas for the teachers. These they confirmed to me as individuals but it was only at the meeting of all the staff that they realized that they all faced the same dilemmas, and they seemed relieved.

There were two dilemmas concerning the children's writing. Firstly, how many of the spelling and grammatical errors should they correct? If they marked them all the children might be discouraged. If they marked few, how would the children ever learn? Secondly, children wrote stories out of their own interests, but some stories were about things the teachers disapproved of and which contradicted ideas of childish innocence. Boys in particular wrote of wars, fighting, and murders. If this disapproval were expressed, and some did so, would this discourage them from writing?

The children's speech presented a similar dilemma. They should be encouraged to express themselves, but should their pronunciation and grammar be corrected, so risking discouraging them? The teachers in any case found that 'there's no time to correct everything they say'.

Teachers looked in vain for some children to show signs of reading readiness and some had concluded that it was better to start pre-reading activities 'as soon as they come. You can't afford to waste time'.

There were dilemmas concerning the children's appearance. The children were not responsible for their being dirty or ill-clothed; however, cleanliness and tidiness were desirable things to the teachers. Most teachers ignored conspicuously dirty hands but insisted that all hands be washed in the context of classroom activities, for example after painting. Public comments on the general dirtiness of children were never made, but there was public praise when one of the habitually dirty appeared clean. Similarly, no teacher remarked publicly on the poor state of children's clothing, but publicly admired a new dress or a boy's 'smart' appearance where this was an improvement.

If news time revealed that some children had had little or no breakfast, teachers would bring milk time forward. When there were extra milks these were saved until the afternoon and given discreetly to those children who were thought to need them most. (News time references to television programmes also revealed how late some children went to bed, as did their tired appearance.)

The children's creative efforts were valued as their own creations, but these were sometimes judged to be below standard for public display. It was tacitly acknowledged among all teachers that they 'improved' these products, redrawing outlines, adding details, and structuring much of the creative process (See Chapter 4).

The children's behaviour was not as good as the teachers would have liked but the children could not be blamed for this. Should they adopt more direct punitive forms of control so denying the notion of the children's innocence? Most did not; they had as much professional equanimity, pleasantness, and affection as any other set of teachers I observed. A consequence was that they ignored some of the poor behaviour in the classroom, admitted to me individually, but only revealed collectively at the meeting.

> Small boy has made a plasticine penis which he holds to his flies to the others' amusement. Some of them call out, 'Winkle!' Others make their own. The teacher sees this, but ignores it.

Distraction was a common ploy.

> Paul and Denis are exchanging short punches. Teacher has seen. 'Paul will you come and do this puzzle for me please?'

But sometimes there was explicit recognition of disapproved behaviour.

> 'I'll get a piece of Sellotape and put it over your mouth if you spit.'

Some expressed the view that they would 'get nothing done' if they spent all their time 'checking' the children's behaviour. Even with suspected stealing, confrontation was avoided.

> The toy cars were counted at the beginning of the afternoon, now one is missing. Teacher asks them to look everywhere, then to look in the coat pockets 'in case it's there. Someone may have put it there'. It is found. She makes no accusations but later admitted that she knows who did it. 'Things often go missing.' She explained that the children have few toys at home. 'The nicer we make it here the worse home seems to them.'

When children first started school they could be 'just like little animals'. In consequence the reception class teachers felt they required 'social training'. 'They have to get adjusted to school before they can start to learn anything.' Many new children could not hold a pencil and few could use scissors. Some did seem to know how to wash their hands, and the infants' helpers were always ready with clean pants for those who wet themselves. 'You have to do nursery education first.' This extract from the H.M.I.'s report of 1936 shows much the same situation.

> Both the headmistress and the staff realise, quite rightly, that in a school of this type, training in good personal and social habits and in speech take an important place.

The consequences in the playground

An extension of this dilemma over behaviour was the playground. Teachers on duty ignored much of the fighting, tripping, and punching that went on, but agreed that playtime was a 'problem'. Some explained this as an effect of watching so much violence on television, a theory confirmed when the children practised karate chops and kicks after the introduction of the Kung Fu series. On Mrs Brown's initiative, climbing apparatus was introduced to provide a more acceptable outlet for the children's energies (the cathartic theory—see Chapter 2). She obtained a large tree trunk and some concrete pipes for them to play around, but these only effectively reduced the problem when the numbers of children were limited, and being on grass they could not be used in the winter.

Another attempt was the introduction of hoops and skipping ropes. For a few days the children played with these in the intended way, but within a week I observed the hoops being used to trip up other children, ropes being whirled over heads and thrown, children tied up, 'everything', I wrote in my notes at the time, 'short of strangulation'. The hoops and ropes were withdrawn. With the reorganization under the Nossex local education authority all first schools dropped the afternoon break, which helped, and Mrs Brown reduced the number of children out on morning break by increasing the number of breaks from two to three.

The consequences—Mrs Brown the headmistress

When Mrs Brown was offered the headship of Burnley Road she was puzzled at being asked by the appointing committee if she would like time to consider her decision to accept. 'They knew what I was taking on.' The nature of what she was taking on had consequences for what she did as headteacher—consequences based on conscious decisions regarding the definition of the children in the school, and of their family and home background.

Mrs Brown's policy regarding relations with parents was 'to get them on our side a bit'. The school had no Parent Teacher Association and Mrs Brown thought that the parents would be unlikely to attend formal meetings and talks. This was partly confirmed when, at the direction of the new Nossex authority, all headteachers were obliged to call a meeting of parents to elect parent-managers. Only one parent attended—and he became a manager. However, the attendance at the two Open Days, held in the afternoons, because they were judged to be more favourable than the evenings, was high (about 85 per cent). Small numbers of mothers helped the children change for swimming, repaired books, and did other jobs, and one helped in Mrs Black's class two afternoons a week.

Mrs Brown had tried a staggered entry scheme so that only a few new children started school on the same day, but mothers brought the children in at the beginning of term or other times, having lost or ignored the appointments sent to them. The scheme was abandoned and all the term's entry came in on the first day. The next day they were all inspected for nits in their hair, so that mothers could not subsequently blame any infestation on the school. This was another consequence of experience.

Jumble sales were abandoned because they received mainly 'rubbish', and some of the customers (not necessarily parents) were stealing. Instead parents, staff, and 'friends of the school' brought in 'decent things'—clothes, shoes, even furniture—which were on display in the secretary's office adjacent to the headteacher's room. Parents could come in anytime to pick up bargains at 10p or 20p—some were even allowed credit or to take things away on approval. Mrs Brown saw this as a way of helping the parents to come into the school (she often emerged from her office for a chat), raising money for the school, and doing the parents 'a good turn'.

Mrs Brown went into the playground in the morning when letting the children in, and again at the end of school to 'put on my smile' and talk to any mothers there. She dealt with any problems involving parents, helping them to fill in free meal applications, advising on health and financial matters, as well as receiving abuse, threats, and, on two occasions, physical attacks. She was the main contact with all of the external agencies, the health visitors, child welfare officers, school doctor, social workers, dentist, audiologist, speech therapist, educational psychologist, social security officers, education officers, education welfare officers, and the police. She summarized this by saying, 'We are really doing social work.'

Because she looked after 'external affairs', her teachers were able to 'get on with the job' without extra worries. Unlike other headteachers she exercised only light control over their teaching methods and activities, demanding no weekly reports or termly plans ('wastes their time'). Although she had her views about classroom practice these were not urged on the teachers. Instead, she made sure they had all the materials and facilities they wanted. She was successful in getting extra money from the local authority and raising it through voluntary efforts such as saving newspapers. Her staff were well pleased in this respect. 'Whatever we want Mrs Brown will get it for us.'

The children of Burnley Road were defined as not very successful academically. It was Mrs Brown's idea to create an alternative success system for them—creative or craft work. An annual exhibition was staged in the entrance of the main library in Newbridge. The preparation for this was spread over a long period of time, and each had a theme, including 'pirates' and 'the sea'. Mrs Brown admitted this was not representative of the year's work, and that it showed more creativity on the part of the teachers than the children, but like the teachers she claimed that the children took pride in the product and had badgered their parents into going to the exhibition, the first time either had been into the library.

Another purpose of the exhibition was to correct the 'image' of the school. In our general survey several teachers made unfavourable remarks about the two Burnley Road schools—usually based on hearsay. Mrs Brown was concerned that when a scale post was vacant she had no applicants from other Newbridge schools. She reported with some satisfaction comments she overheard at the exhibition, expressing astonishment at the origin of the work ('What there!'). She gladly put up with the 'catty' remarks her fellow headteachers made about her 'gimmicks' following her appearance on television and reports in the local paper.

The exhibitions and the generous provision of materials were also part of her efforts to maintain the morale of the staff—efforts that were clearly fulfilled. They trusted and respected Mrs Brown, and some of them privately feared what would happen if she went. Relationships between the teachers seemed good with few jealousies and little backbiting. Most lunched together in a local pub every Wednesday, and there was a Christmas lunch with wine. Staff turnover was mainly due to their husbands moving, or, as with Mrs Pink, pregnancy.

Being the teacher at Burnley Road

Being a teacher at Burnley Road was not easy. The experience of children in the classroom was often at variance with their child-centred ideologies. The family–home background theory only enabled them to explain why the children's behaviour and progress were not as they should be, but did not explain them away. The theory helped to preserve their identities as good infants' teachers but did not stop them feeling that this identity was threatened. They feared that outsiders who did not 'know' the children and their backgrounds would judge them on the children's behaviour and progress. Because of the gap between what their ideologies defined children to be and the way the children 'were' they anxiously held on to their own professional standards for children's work and behaviour even when these were not always fulfilled.

> The teacher's maths display includes a green rhombus, an organge trapezium, and a pink parallelogram. I asked her if any of the children will be doing anything about these shapes. She replied, 'No, but they should.'

Many of the teachers were themselves mothers. Their censure of the behaviour of some children's parents was partly indignation at the presumed consequences this had for what they thought of as the children's well-being. It was also to affirm their own definition of what a parent should be.

CHAPTER TWELVE

Seaton Park School—'Bouncy' Children and 'Nice' Children

Towards the end of my year at Burnley Road I asked the headmistress of Seaton Park school, Mrs Baker, if I could begin visiting her school after the summer holidays. I had gone to Burnley Road knowing it to be the most working-class infants' school in Newbridge. In Seaton Park I hoped to find a school of similar size with a predominantly middle-class composition. After a short time in the school I discovered this was not the case. However, I decided to continue, a decision I did not regret.

My mistake was due to the changing nature of Seaton Park school. It was opened in 1956 as a combined junior and infants' school, but an expanding population lead to the setting up of a separate junior school. My information about the social composition of Seaton Park was based on data from this school obtained in the survey of 1972, and referring to pupils who had left the previous year. What I only subsequently found out was that the catchment area of both schools had been considerably increased so altering their social compositions.

Seaton Park infants' was a single-storey building with twelve large classrooms, a hall, and a dining-room, set in a large, grassy area partly shared with a neighbouring comprehensive school. The houses in the area were mainly of the same post-war period as the school. These were of two kinds, owner-occupied (mainly semi-detached) and short terraces of council houses. These latter were not in distinct areas but confined to particular roads. As a stranger it was sometimes difficult to spot the changes in housing class when moving through the area. The council houses were varied in their construction. Their gardens were generally as well kept as those of adjoining owner-occupied houses.

The Census data, based upon the correct catchment area, show the social composition of the area to be less working class than that of Burnley Road (Chapter 9). This would be partly due to the owner-occupied element, but the council houses' tenants were locally regarded as 'better' than those in the Burnley Road area where, by the Newbridge council policy, any 'bad' tenants were housed.

It was inevitable that I should compare what I saw at Seaton Park with that at Burnley Road. The similarities between them (and the Langley school) are what I take to be typical of most infant or first schools, and these have been described in earlier chapters. The differences I observed in the classrooms of the schools may be partly explained in terms of the physical differences between the schools and the differences between the styles of the headmistresses. However, my major explanation is based upon the differences in the way the teachers defined the children they taught: different definitions with different consequences, but with interesting similarities in terms of the teachers' explanatory 'theories' of why the children 'were as they were'.

I was able to observe all 14 class teachers at Burnley Road. There were twelve at Seaton Park but I was only able to observe nine of them. At Mrs Baker's request I did not go into the classroom of a teacher having 'problems' in her first year of teaching. Another left to be replaced by a temporary teacher who knew less about the school than I did. By bad management a third had a student teacher in the class for teaching practice at the time I was able to observe.

As at Burnley Road I gave my account of their definitions and my theory of their 'theories' to all the teachers. After the first meeting, with Mrs Baker present, they were enthusiastic enough for a second, which Mrs Baker could not attend. Only one of them dissented from my basic presentation, upon which the following is substantially based. Significantly she was the temporary teacher. The other teachers seemed to agree with the one who told her at the meeting, 'Just wait till you've been here a bit longer.'

Defining the children

As an extension of their typifying individual children the teachers also typified 'the children in this school'. Their shared definition of most children was that they were about average for their progress in school work, perhaps capable of doing better if they were to 'concentrate' more. They were not badly behaved or difficult to manage although 'a bit of a handful at times'. They tended to be 'lively' or 'bouncy', 'full of themselves', unable to 'sit still for five minutes'. They were untidy and careless about the contents of the classroom. They could sometimes be very demanding of the teacher's attention. As a rider to any discussion about 'the children in this school', all the teachers added phrases such as 'Of course, we do have some nice children'. The nature of these 'nice' children will be dealt with later.

The typification of 'most children in this school' was constructed and made 'real' out of the teachers' own experiences with the children, compared with other experiences, and shared privately with the other teachers. The children (and their parents) were discussed in the staff-room, but less than at Burnley Road.

The children's work progress was assessed continuously. Its 'average' nature was confirmed 'objectively'. The school did not use a single reading scheme as at Burnley Road (or Langley). Mrs Baker felt that teachers should use the scheme they felt 'happiest with'. Some teachers used more than one scheme in the same class. Mrs Baker monitored the children's progress by means of a reading test she administered after about a year in school, since there was no simple significance attached to which book the child was reading. The teachers mentioned the scores of individual children in commenting upon them in general. The mean reading quotient, using the Schonell Test, was 94, rather below average (girls 96, boys 91). (The Young Test gave a mean of 90.4—girls 97.1, boys 84.0—a much larger sex gap. None of these mean scores was known to the teachers.) However, teachers did sometimes proudly point out a child with a high reading age.

Teachers did sometimes refer to the limited range of the children's writing and drawings, but not to the same extent as at Burnley Road. They did not show concern about the children's ability to express themselves. Only six children were in the records as having been referred to the speech therapist. Children asked questions of the teacher more often than those at Burnley Road, and in 'discussions' displayed more 'everyday knowledge', although the range of this was sometimes commented upon. There were too many references to television for some teachers' liking. The children suffered from 'tellyitis', so limiting their range of useful experiences.

The children's 'bouncy' or 'lively' classroom behaviour did not include the spitting, punching or kicking sometimes observed at Burnley Road. I saw a few pinches and nudges, and a few slyly poked tongues. The children sometimes sang television jingles, but I heard no obscenities. Lining up at the door or sitting down for story time were not often the occasions for scuffles. No one fell over deliberately during music and movement, or 'accidently' tripped others up. There was no concern over their behaviour at playtime. The outdoor apparatus was there for them to play on to 'develop their skills and confidence', not to provide acceptable outlets for their energies, as at Burnley Road. The same action can have different subjective meanings.

Their 'liveliness' or 'bounciness' took the form of chattering and frequent movements around the classroom. Many children seemed to be able to complete tasks such as painting, drawing, writing, and doing mathematics whilst chattering and laughing most of the time. But they always stopped when asked, and did not usually chat whilst listening to the teacher or a story or watching schools' television. The teachers felt the older ones would do better at their work if they did not talk so much. The quiet hum was not always quiet enough.

The mobility of the children was at least in part permitted by the large size of the classrooms. Many teachers followed Mrs Baker's policy of allowing the children to 'work' as well as play on the floor. This did not often lead to upsets between the children, no one seemed to tread on fingers deliberately, but the teachers felt the children would get more done if they wandered around less.

As they chattered and wandered the children seemed to the teachers to be neglectful of the contents of the classroom. They did not always pick up things knocked over accidentally; they tended to get out another plaything without putting the first away. They lacked 'the social graces' and there was not enough 'please' and 'thank you'. They were 'careless' with books, holding them by the pages or the cover. However, I heard of no case of a child stealing anything.

By comparison with Burnley Road there was no idea that the boys' behaviour posed a particular problem; they were just 'silly' more often than the girls.

The origins of 'bounciness'

The 'liveliness' or 'bounciness' of 'most children in this school' was not such a problem for the teachers at Seaton Park as was the definition of the children held by those at Burnley Road. Nevertheless, it required explanation and, as at Burnley Road, there was a family–home background theory. The children were as they were because of the way their parents had brought them up. The homes were defined as materially well provided for. The parents 'spoilt' or indulged the children, who 'always get what they want', and were allowed to 'do whatever they like' and 'get their own way'. Hence their chattering, wandering, lack of respect for property, untidiness, and demands for attention. Their homes had few books and their parents held narrow interests. Hence the children's 'limited' knowledge, except of television where 'they watch anything and everything'. 'The trouble is that they forget there's a switch on the side.' This typification was constructed by the teachers drawing upon their observations and experience of both the children and their parents.

In the whole of Seaton Park there were only two children who were as dirty and poorly dressed as many were at Burnley Road. These were sisters who received a great deal of sympathy from their teachers and Mrs Baker. Seaton Park had a school uniform which approximately a quarter of the children wore to some extent. Mrs Brown at Burnley Road explained that the parents there could not afford to buy uniforms even if one existed.

Most of the children at Seaton Park were clean, healthy-looking, and well dressed. On this account their parents were seen as 'caring'. Their clothes, particularly the girls', were sometimes miniature versions of adult fashions of which some teachers obliquely disapproved.

> Carole is wearing sling-back, platform shoes which look like those of her mother, who has just left her. Teacher, rather coldly: 'Mind you don't fall in those, Carole.'

Some teachers remarked on the expensive nature of some of the children's clothes, the mothers among them knowing their price in the Newbridge shops.

Children were allowed, but not encouraged, to bring their own toys to school. After Christmas they brought expensive toys and games which they admired among themselves. The teachers privately disapproved of many of these, publicly showing polite but unenthusiastic interest in such things as talking or walking dolls.

The children sometimes brought their own books into school, which the teachers often defined as unsuitable, for example the 'Man from Uncle' annual, and reported that the children were disappointed when they were not read to the class. The teachers noted how the children often lost interest in the things they brought from home, leaving them about the room and losing them. This careless affluence toys was matched by pocket money. Its loss in school lead some teachers to collect it in at the beginning of the day for safe-keeping. They remarked on the amounts. 'Nearly a pound for a 5-year-old.'

Seaton Park had a curious institution called 'lunch'. Originally this was an apple bought and eaten at milk time. Following an apple shortage, packets of biscuits were substituted, and later crisps. Children also brought along their own 'lunch', which the teachers noted were often expensive sweets and chocolates, which sometimes the children threw away without finishing.

News and news time revealed the extent of the 'tellyitis' of the children, and how limited, in the teachers' opinions, was the range of their experiences.

> 'If you asked any of them who went out of Newbridge at the weekend it would probably be none.'

A teacher's first encounter with parents was sometimes actually in the home. It was Mrs Baker's policy to release teachers during the day to take the admission slip to the parents of any child due to enter school the next term. She encouraged them to write their impressions of the home for the child's file, but only a few did.

> Mother appeared interested and cooperative—a good clean home.

> Here is a very good home with a very good mother. There are three children of which Gray is the second. The 2-year-old baby girl Tracey was asleep on the sofa. There was a little black dog—beautifully clean.

There was sometimes a little social apprehension of these home visits but no teacher expressed fear of parents as at Burnley Road. Following the home visit the parents had the opportunity to bring their child for a visit to school before officially starting. This too was observed and sometimes noted by the teachers.

> Very shy and tearful—wouldn't leave Mum. Immature, sheltered? Hard to settle. Needs drawing out?

Parents and their children were also observed on a daily basis. Each classroom had its own external entrance through a window wall and parents could be seen outside collecting and leaving their children. The mothers were commonly dressed in slightly dated, fairly smart casual wear, not unlike the teachers. The fathers (rarely seen at Burnley Road) were often moustached and trendily dressed. Young children were sometimes brought into or collected from the classroom by a parent, and the teachers disapprovingly observed the parents remove their child's coat or do it up, fetch it from or hang it up in the cloakroom area. This 'spoiling' or 'molly-coddling' accounted for the children's carelessness, 'They never do anything for themselves', and the inability of some of them to do up buttons or even dress themselves after apparatus work. However, no teacher complained about their toilet habits.

Special occasions provided further opportunities to observe parents. These notes were written after the Christmas Carol Concert, one of three performances bringing in nearly 500 guests.

> Some parents could easily be taken for teachers in dress and general appearance. The audience is much quieter than at Burnley Road. They talk among themselves quietly. No loud voices calling out across to one another. They respond to the decorations and the Christmas tree but most of all to their own children, craning their necks to see them, smiling, even giving little waves. Some children reciprocate. Unlike Burnley Road the teachers do not express disapproval or dissociation from the audience. There is a nice selection of traditional nans in warm coats, fur hats, and glasses. Outside there are at least 50 cars parked.

These parents were not neglectful in the teachers' opinion. They wanted to help their children's education but 'needed education themselves'.

Their efforts to help were shown in some children coming to school able to write their names, but, to the teachers' disapproval, in block capitals. Some were thought to be anxious to the point of 'pushing' their children. Teachers allowed children to take their reading books home but had reservations about the way some were 'drilled' by their parents. The mother who wrote this letter was judged to be 'over-anxious'.

Dear Mrs Smith,
Would it be possible to come and see you about Madeline's reading. I am getting very concerned about it, also it is worrying her. My other children attended Seaton Park school and by the time they were Madeline's age they were reading very well.
Yours sincerely,
J. Crisp (Mrs.)

These definitions of 'most children in this school', 'the families and home background of most children in this school', and the way they were assumed to be causally related, were shared among the teachers, who compared them with other relevant experiences.

They sometimes expressed concern about the number of children one-parent families, due to separation and divorce, but without the strong moral censure of teachers at Burnley Road. But then there was no talk or 'evidence' of 'fancymen' or 'boyfriends'. They did express some mild disapproval of what they felt was the materialism of many parents, who 'boasted' of their new cars and foreign holidays. This was sometimes obliquely expressed in public, with a tinge of bitter envy.

Teacher conducting class prayers in the hall asks the children, 'Who watched the royal wedding on television?' Virtually all the children's hands go up. 'Who watched it on colour television?' Most hands go up. 'Which teachers watched on colour television?' she says half-jokingly with a meaning edge to it. Some of her colleagues react to her meaning, but none put up their hands.

As at Burnley Road, the family–home background theory absolved the children from responsibility for their shortcomings, so preserving their innocence, and the teachers too, so leaving the child-centred methods unquestioned.

My observations at Seaton Park were affected by those at Burnley Road. I looked for incidents in the former that I had seen in the latter, and I was able to make comparisons in a way that none of the teachers could. By fortunate coincidence a student teacher who had been at Burnley Road on teaching practice whilst I was there was also at Seaton Park the following year. I took the opportunity to ask her to compare the two schools and was pleased to find that her 'pictures' of the children and 'impressions' of the teachers were similar to my own observations.

The consequences of the definition

The 'real' consequences of defining the children as tending to be untidy, to show lack of respect for property, and to be 'short on good manners' were that the teachers consciously stressed tidiness, respect for property, and politeness in their exercise of social control in the classroom.

> Teacher: 'I don't want any rubbish on the floor. Where does the rubbish go?' Pupils' chorus: 'In the dustbin.'

> 'Now this is a lovely new book and I don't want to see it left on the floor for people to walk all over.'

> 'We'll have our news. Remember our rule. Only one person at a time.'

The definition of the children as having a limited range of useful experiences had two consequences. Numerous educational visits were made to farms, factories, museums, and 'other interesting places'. These were intended to extend the children's experience and formed the basis of projects and follow-up written and craft work. I heard no reports of children not going on such trips because of financial problems. The children of Burnley Road were also defined as lacking useful experiences by their teachers but very few educational visits were arranged, because it was found difficult to get the parents to pay for them, either because they were unwilling or unable.

The second consequence was the teachers' emphasis upon 'stretching the children's imagination'. This was done through stories. I heard more involving magic, fantasy, and fairies read aloud in Seaton Park than elsewhere. The follow-up activities of painting and writing their own stories were also part of this. Music and movement were valued in this way too.

The definition of the children as being 'about average in their progress' did not lead to the creation of an 'adjustment class' or special 'extra reading' arrangements as at Burnley Road. Children with low reading ages detected by Mrs Baker did receive extra help in the classroom. No alternative success system was introduced. Although the children 'could do better', improvement in their work was thought to be dependent on their improving their behaviour and widening their experiences.

Some of Mrs Baker's actions as headmistress could be seen as consequences of the definition the children and their parents. The parents were defined as being interested in their children's education but as not knowing how to be of the greatest help. Mrs Baker's home–school policy was to mobilize this interest usefully.

A P.T.A. had existed before Mrs Baker had arrived 2 years before but attendances of meetings were small and so she had disbanded it, feeling that having to join it was a barrier to some parents. However, open invitations to talks about education, and opportunities to try out the 'new' mathematics were not well attended. But events like the Harvest Festival, Christmas Carol Concert, and jumble sale were always packed. Parents could attend the school prayers in the hall, and a few usually did so, often to see their own children perform. She was disappointed in her efforts to mobilize mothers' help in the classroom; some were willing but few were defined as able. A teacher described a mother who had come to 'help' with the class Christmas party as 'standing around, looking on, and smoking'.

Unlike Mrs Brown at Burnley Road, Mrs Baker did not feel she had to protect her teachers from the parents, and when teachers and parents met they seemed to relate as social equals, indeed some teachers thought some parents showed lack of respect to Mrs Baker. They were 'full of themselves like their children'.

'Nice' children from 'good homes'

As a rider to their definition of 'most children in this school', all the teachers added that they did have some 'really nice' children who had by implication the characteristics that in the teachers' view children should have. One teacher called them 'normal' children. These were the sort of children who were sometimes proudly pointed out to have high reading ages, to be polite, well behaved, and have a respect for property. The books they brought in from home were Mrs Pepperpot stories and A. A. Milne, not Scooby-Doo annuals.

The teachers were not very explicit about the 'good homes' these children came from. This is consistent with my previous analysis. When teachers defined children as being different from how they should be, they looked for evidence in their homes and family lives to explain the difference. These 'nice' children were as children should be, and needed little explanation. Two clues were offered. In talking about these children reference was occasionally made to the father's and/or mother's occupation, most commonly that of teacher or lecturer.

> Charming parents. Mother and father, both teachers, came. Most interested in everything and I think they will be very cooperative. The little girl settled, knew someone in my class. Didn't want to go home. (Teacher's notes on pre-school visit to classroom)

Reference was also made to the road the child lived in and the type of housing.

> Private semi-detached. Well looked after, clean and tidy. Good home. Mrs Jones very concerned that Heather (only daughter) should have the best education possible. Determined to give every help in anyway. Anxious to cooperate with school needs. (Teacher's notes on home visit)

As a consequence of their home visits and other sources of information most teachers had a good knowledge of the local social geography. One teacher reported she looked at the addresses of the new children 'to get some idea of what's coming'. Mrs Baker was perhaps the most knowledgeable about this and could classify every road in the neighbourhood into owner-occupied or council-tenanted. She reported some conflict between the owner occupiers and council tenants when they met as parents. The former were 'stand-offish' and would not talk to the others.

From the children's addresses it was possible to classify most of them according to housing class. Ignoring those whose status was not clear, 35 per cent were from owner-occupied housing (higher than most teachers estimated) and 65 per cent from council housing. From the records of fathers' occupations (not known for all children) it was possible to show, unsurprisingly, that most (90 per cent) of council tenants were working class, but, a little less expected, 24 per cent of owner occupiers were working class. (For this purpose working class refers to manual occupations, middle class to non-manual.)

The teachers were reluctant to equate 'nice children' and 'good homes' with middle classness and owner occupiers. Mrs Baker was very keen that the teachers should keep records about the children which included an assessment of 'home environment'. Unfortunately these were not made for all children, but on the basis of the teachers' informal comments about families it was possible to classify their written remarks as being either favourable, unfavourable, mixed or neutral. The most common criterion was the level of parental interest. Three examples are:

Favourable: 'Good. Mother interested in Sally's progress.'

Mixed/neutral: 'Interested mother, rather anxious at first until he began to read.'

Unfavourable: 'Not much interest, never comes to ask about child.'

Of the twelve teachers in the school nine gave more favourable ratings to the homes of the middle-class children in their care, two gave more to the homes of working-class children, and one had an even distribution. Nine teachers also gave more favourable ratings to the 'home environment' of owner occupiers, only one gave more to council homes, and two rated them equally. Table 7 shows the overall distribution for all children (where the data were available) and all teachers.

More owner-occupied homes were rated favourably than council house homes, and slightly more middle-class than working-class homes. These illustrate the teachers' reluctance to equate 'good homes' with being owner-occupied or middle class. If this were so the differences in percentages would be

Table 7 Teachers' comments on children's 'home environment' (percentages)

	Comment		
Housing Class	Favourable	Mixed/ neutral	Unfavourable
Owner-occupied (n = 90)	70.0	23.3	6.7
Council tenant (n = 165)	38.8	35.8	25.5
Social class by father's occupation			
Middle class (n = 72)	59.7	30.6	9.7
Working class (n = 98)	51.0	35.7	13.3

greater. However, 'good homes' were more commonly middle class, and especially more often owner-occupied.

These figures do not show that teachers defined 'good homes', or any other kind, simply on the basis of housing class or the father's occupation. The home visit, giving knowledge of the former, occurred before the child's school career began, and few mentioned the jobs of children's fathers. 'Good homes', as those receiving favourable comments in the records, were judged largely on the level of parental interest assessed through direct contact with the parents, both informally and at formal parents' meetings. 'Good homes' were those of 'interested parents' and their being more often middle class and owner occupiers was partly incidental to this typification.

Who were the 'nice children'? On the Newbridge record card teachers were required to assess each child's 'conduct' and 'attitude to school work'. I have already referred to these in discussing the way teachers typified boys and girls (Chapter 7). There I showed that in all three schools girls were on average more favourably rated than boys. This has two implications for this discussion. Firstly, if 'nice children' received more favourable ratings, then girls were more often 'nice children' than boys. Secondly, it follows that sex differences cannot be ignored in comparing children from different backgrounds. Thus the comparisons should be between boys from middle-class homes with boys from working-class homes, and middle-class girls with working-class girls. The number in each of these categories was very small in each classroom, so that the ratings made by individual teachers were too small for statistical analysis, particularly in view of the missing data, so that an analysis, was only possible of all the teachers' ratings of all the children.

Table 8 shows that girls received more favourable ratings than boys from the same housing or social class backgrounds, and that children from owner-occupied and from middle-class homes were more favourably rated than children

Table 8 Teachers' ratings of children's 'conduct' and 'attitude to work' by sex, housing, and social class

| | Boys | | | Girls | | |
	Favour-able %	Unfavour-able %	(n)	Favour-able %	Unfavour-able %	(n)
'Conduct'						
Owner-occupied	45.0	20.0	(40)	73.3	5.8	(60)
Council tenancy	19.4	24.5	(98)	47.3	7.3	(110)
Middle class	39.3	14.3	(28)	73.5	2.9	(34)
Working class	27.7	27.7	(47)	55.7	9.8	(61)
'Attitude to work'						
Owner-occupied	48.7	21.6	(37)	58.9	1.8	(56)
Council tenancy	16.1	29.0	(93)	41.0	11.4	(105)
Middle class	46.2	15.4	(26)	63.6	6.1	(33)
Working class	15.2	30.4	(46)	45.6	7.0	(57)

of the same sex from council house and from working-class homes. Thus the most favourably rated were girls from owner-occupied or middle-class homes, the least favourably rated were boys from council house or working-class homes.

These figures do not show that teachers assessed children on the basis of their sex and housing or social class backgrounds. I have described in Chapter 7 how teachers typified children on the basis of day-to-day interactions and observations in the classroom. These figures are my creations, and until I gave versions of them to the teachers at Seaton Park (at the suggestion of Mrs Baker) they were not aware of the patterns of their assessments in this kind of way. Interestingly, the same predominant pattern was also found for the reading quotients of children, based upon standardized tests administered by Mrs Baker independently of the teachers. The mean score for middle-class girls was the highest at 101, middle-class boys and working-class girls had the same mean score of 97, and working-class boys the lowest at 87. The significance of all of these figures will be returned to later.

In addition it must not be assumed that 'good homes' were most commonly the middle-class and owner-occupied ones that girls came from. Table 9 shows that the teachers' evaluations showed none of the obvious sex differences of their assessments of the children. This suggests that teachers evaluated the children's homes independently of the sex of the child.

'Nice children from good homes' was part of the teachers' 'family–home background theory' to explain some, but not all, of the variation in children's progress and behaviour. Table 10 shows that children whose 'home environments' were favourably assessed by the teachers were also more likely to receive favourable assessments for 'conduct' and 'attitude to work', the converse being broadly the case for unfavourable assessments.

These figures do not 'prove' the 'theory' to be 'correct'. They are a crude illustration of the 'family–home background theory' being confirmed by the actions of the teachers who posed it. They do not necessarily show that teacher assessed the children on the basis of their (the teachers') definition of their social backgrounds. I have already described how teachers searched for background 'evidence' to make an acceptable explanation of a child's poor progress or behaviour (Chapter 7).

Table 9 Teachers' comments on 'home environment' by children's sex, housing, and social class

| | Boys | | | Girls | | |
	Favour-able %	Unfavour-able %	(n)	Favour-able %	Unfavour-able %	(n)
Owner-occupied	72.7	12.1	(33)	68.4	3.5	(57)
Council tenant	37.7	29.0	(69)	39.6	22.9	(96)
Middle class	56.3	15.6	(32)	62.5	5.0	(40)
Working class	50.0	12.5	(40)	51.7	13.8	(58)

Table 10 Teachers' comments on 'home environment' and ratings of 'conduct' and 'attitude to work'

Home	n	'Conduct' Favour- able	Mixed/ neutral	Unfavour- able	Chi square
Favourable	118	55.1	37.3	7.6	23.1
Mixed/neutral	63	38.1	50.8	11.1	p 0.001
Unfavourable	40	20.1	50.0	30.0	4 df
		'Attitude to work' (%)			
Favourable	107	49.5	43.0	7.5	39.4
Mixed/neutral	58	22.4	60.3	17.2	p 0.001
Unfavourable	38	23.7	31.6	44.7	4 df

I have made many reservations about the figures presented from the Seaton Park records. Individual teachers, constrained by the structure of the record sheets and the expectations of the headmistress, assessed individual children, but not all the children were completely assessed. I classified the children's social backgrounds from information recorded by their parents, and I categorized the teachers' assessments in accord with their classroom practices. Because of the missing data and the small number of children in each category in each school class, most of my calculations were of the total sample of children, an artificial statistical aggregate or group, which never had a social existence in a single classroom. In addition, the aggregate was not a constant one. This all illustrates the limitations of 'found' or 'discovered' data. Had I used a questionnaire the 'created' data probably would have been more complete, but more an outcome of my actions and not the teachers'.

Why, having made all these reservations, did I decide to report these figures? Artificial, incomplete, and remote as they are from events in the classrooms, they all show a consistent pattern of variations by sex and social background. This pattern explains nothing, it must be explained if it has any social significance. I created the pattern again from data at the Langley school, described in the next chapter, and a consideration of its social significance will be made in Chapters 14 and 15.

CHAPTER THIRTEEN

The Langley School—The 'Anxious to Please' Children

'We have 75 per cent professional families.' Miss Fox, the headmistress, made this reference to the catchment of the Langley school on my first visit which I made to ask her to allow me to continue my observations there. I knew at the time that no catchment area in Newbridge would have so high a proportion of 'professionals' by the usual sociological definitions, but the special significance of her comment only became clear later.

Within a few weeks of my observations at the Seaton Park school I decided I would have to extend my research to a third school with a more middle-class intake. Because I wanted the size of the schools to be as close as possible, my choice was limited to two. Towards the end of my time at Seaton Park I knew that it would have to be the Langley school. The alternative, although more middle class in composition, had a mixed catchment area of expensive owner-occupied houses and 'better' council houses, a mixture similar to that of Seaton Park. (The most middle-class schools in Newbridge were small and situated at the edge of the administrative area.) The Langley area was almost exclusively owner-occupied housing but, as I have already explained in Chapter 9, drew children from outside the official catchment area who may have increased its middle classness.

The buildings of the Langley school were mainly Edwardian with later, post-Second World War, additions. The Langley elementary school was opened in 1908. Following the 1944 Education Act a new secondary modern school was built on an adjacent site leaving the building to the junior and infants' schools. The modern school was closed during the reorganization of secondary education in Newbridge, and the new buildings taken over by the middle school created from the junior school. This left the newly created first school in possession of the original building. Unlike Burnley Road or Seaton Park, the Langley school did not have a grassy surround, but the basic two-storey building had overall more internal space than the other schools, with wider corridors and useful storage places, although the classrooms were, with one exception, all smaller than those at Seaton Park, and a few were smaller than those at Burnley Road.

The area immediately around the school was of owner-occupied terraced houses of the same period. Beyond these were pockets of post-war, semi-detached, owner-occupied houses and a few substantial older detached properties. The children from outside the official catchment area mainly came from a more recent estate of semi-detached, owner-occupied houses.

The purpose of my going to the Langley school was to compare what I saw with my observations at Seaton Park and Burnley Road. The similarities between them are what I have taken to be typical of most infant or first schools, and these have been described in earlier chapters. The differences I observed may be partly explained in terms of the physical differences between the schools and the differences in the styles of the headmistresses, but my major explanation, as before, is based upon the way the teachers defined the children they taught. I was able to observe 15 of the 16 teachers; Mrs Fox asked me not to go into the classroom of a probationer who was 'having some trouble'. I had two meetings with all the teachers in which I presented a version of the analysis made here.

Most of my research was based upon my lone observations, and I am well aware of all the reservations that are made about this method. I therefore welcomed any opportunities for some corroboration. I have already mentioned the student teacher who had teaching practice in both the Burnley Road and Seaton Park schools. At the Langley school there was a teacher, Mrs Lamb, who had taught at Seaton Park until recently, and I took the opportunity to tape a conversation with her about the two schools. I mentioned David Hartley's work on sex differences at Burnley and Langley in Chapter 7. I deliberately refrained from talking in detail about my work to him at first, and only compared general observations when he had substantially completed his own field work; in these we were in good accord. In 1975 Burnley Road was included in a sample of schools visited by a team of H.M.I.'s in connection with a national enquiry. The inspectors informally suggested that some of the teachers should visit other schools in the area. In consequence one teacher, Mrs Silver, spent a day at the Langley school, after which David Hartley taped an interview with her. Mrs Lamb and Mrs Silver's comparisons of two sets of school were very valuable and I shall quote them later. However, only I was able to compare all three schools. I tried to understand each school in terms of the teachers' actions, and to delineate the social principles behind these by the process of comparison. There is no way of knowing whether my conclusions would have been different if I had observed the schools in a different order.

Defining the children

Teachers at the Langley school held a common definition of 'the children in this school' constructed from their individual observations and assessments of the children they taught. They were 'bright children', 'anxious to please', 'well behaved'. 'There's nothing I can grumble about them really.'

Their general 'brightness' was demonstrated daily to the teachers. They were judged to be able to express themselves clearly and 'always have plenty to say for themselves', and the older ones 'have plenty to say and plenty to write'. (Only six children were in the records as having been to the speech therapist.) They had a 'good general knowledge'; when asking questions the teachers could be sure 'someone will know'. They were judged to have a stock of useful experiences to draw upon. At news time the request, 'Did anyone do anything exciting over the weekend', brought such acceptable responses as a visit to a local castle, a walk in the woods or a visit to a stamp exhibition.

Teachers read books to 5-year-olds chapter by chapter, and they demonstrated to their teachers' satisfaction that they had followed the story from day to day, an ability that teachers at Burnley Road doubted many of their 7-year-olds had.

The Fletcher mathematics scheme was used throughout the school. The signal to the teachers of the 'brightness' of the children was the way virtually all the rising eights graduated to the second series books intended for junior school work. The Gay Way reading scheme was used in the school and children's reading progress was marked by their ascent through the books.

The Young Reading Test given to the rising eights gave a mean reading quotient of 100.6 (girls 102.9, boys 98.7). These are average scores and so it is perhaps a little puzzling that the children were thought to be generally good at reading. However, no teacher or Miss Fox saw or calculated a mean R.Q. Miss Fox prepared a complete list of children with their quotients and each teacher was told those of the children in her class. A simple inspection of these apparently confirmed their definition of the children's ability. Miss Fox was well satisfied with their performance. The tests had been introduced by the new Nossex authority who gave the average results for schools in their area the year before, the last before the reorganization of the local authorities. This average was presented in terms of the proportion of children with R.Q.'s above 100. In addition, they gave the proportion for the highest-scoring school in the former authority. Miss Fox was delighted to find that Langley had done better. Unfortunately, when I checked, I found her sums were wrong; she had counted in those scoring 100 as well, but I thought it best not to tell her. Even so, Langley was probably among the higher-scoring schools in the area, certainly higher than both Burnley Road and Seaton Park. Miss Fox gave the children with scores below 100 the Burt Reading Test about a term later and was assured that most had improved.

Mrs Silver compared the children of Burnley Road with those of Langley school.

'The children at Langley were, seem to be, much more articulate, were able to understand and read written instructions. When I talked to them they were very mature and understanding, and even in the reception class they would question and answer very easily. And ours; very impoverished language really.

'We only have two or three children with a reading age of over 10, which means that they are very fluent, and going on the standard of reading of the books they read at our school most of these seemed to read the same sort of books as these children. So I imagine that a lot of their reading ages are about 10 or 11. Something like that.

'And the maths too. They were working on a scheme that we use, but not all the time, and they were far higher, much more advanced and they were reading, very, very complicated instructions and just getting on with it. Whereas our children, even the brighter children come out all the time, whether it is for reassurance or for what, but they don't seem capable of reading through a page and doing what it says without coming up and asking me about it.'

Mrs Lamb found the children at Seaton Park 'not as able' as those at Langley. When she first arrived at Langley,

'I hadn't any experience of these brighter children. I mean, I've never got Seaton Park to the stage these have got.'

The behaviour of children in the classrooms at Langley school was not defined as a problem by the teachers. When they arrived in the morning they quietly sat in their places. At Burnley Road the teachers always had something prepared for the children to do immediately they arrived otherwise 'you'd never get them settled down'. During music and movement no one tripped up other children, or deliberately ran round the wrong way bashing into others and extravagantly falling over, as sometimes happened at Burnley Road. No one made self-consciously 'silly' faces or gestures as at Seaton Park. When a child fell off her chair another helped her up and picked up the chair, asking her if she was all right. A similar incident at Seaton Park evoked laughter and no help. At Burnley Road I observed a few incidents of a child removing a chair so that another fell on the floor. As I watched a small girl gently stroke another's pigtail at the Langley school, I recalled incidents of hair-pulling at Burnley Road.

The playground of Langley was noisy, but although I saw some pushing and pulling of coats, there was no fighting. Even in cold weather many children sat or stood against the walls talking, a rare sight at either Burnley Road or Seaton Park.

Mrs Lamb compared the behaviour of Seaton Park children unfavourably with those at Langley, describing the former as 'almost running up the walls'. Mrs Silver commented on the behaviour of the reception class children.

'They [the teachers] just said, "All right, it's toilet time", and they all stood up and quietly made two lines and walked quietly over and stood in their lines while they all went to the toilet, all 35 of them, and walked back again. I imagine it would be chaos if we tried to do that . . . getting our children to line up to go anywhere is very difficult . . . you know for prayers and things like that, it's a battle to get them to wait quietly.'

She commented to on a particular incident in which a boy at Langley was reproved for jumping up and down on the spot.

'Well nobody [at Burnley Road] would have thought twice about it. It would have been normal sort of behaviour.'

Tidiness was not defined as a problem. Mrs Lamb noticed the difference from Seaton Park.

'It was terribly difficult to keep equipment nice and tidy in your room. Here I have no bother at all.'

Although generally satisfied with the behaviour of most children the teachers at the Langley school did not define them all as paragons; they did not rate all children A for conduct on the school records. Although boys were given less favourable ratings than girls (Chapter 7) they were not regarded as being the special nuisances of the class, as at Burnley Road, nor was there concern about the subject-matter of their drawings or writing. Two teachers actually expressed the wish that some boys could be more 'boyish' and 'have a bit more spirit'.

As at Seaton Park and Burnley Road every teacher 'built a picture' of every individual child she taught. These typifications included 'noisy', 'untidy', 'slow', and 'lazy' children, which differed from that of 'the children in the school', but in the teachers' usage were not incompatible with it.

The 'family–home background theory'

At Burnley Road and Seaton Park the teachers posed a 'family–home background theory' to explain the way 'the children in this school' were. I had expected to hear a similar 'theory' mentioned by teachers or discussed in the staff-room at the Langley school. However, individual teachers said little about the children's homes and families unless I asked them, and I never heard any general discussion about home backgrounds in the staff-room. Individual children were mentioned over coffee but usually in affectionate anecdotes about the 'funny' things they said or did. Mrs Lamb agreed that they felt very little curiosity about the children's homes and seldom discussed them, unlike her former colleagues at Seaton Park.

The significance of Miss Fox's comment, 'We have 75 per cent professional families', was that she and the teachers' conceptions of the children's homes were vague but favourable.

Unlike Mrs Brown at Burnley Road, Miss Fox did not let the teachers know details about family problems which came her way.

> 'I keep them in here. [Taps head.] It's nobody's business whose husband has left them or who had a baby without being married.'

On her instructions notes about parents separating or other changes in family circumstance were not put in the children's files.

The teachers' lack of curiosity is consistent with the theory I have posed. At Burnley Road and, to a lesser extent, Seaton Park, the teachers' definition of 'children in this school' required explanation because it was discrepant with the definition of children based upon their child-centred ideologies. The 'family–home background theory' preserved these ideologies and the consonant definition of children as innocent; the blame was on the parents, not the teachers or children. At the Langley school the teachers' definition of 'children in this school' was very close to the definition based upon their ideologies. The children were in general as they were expected to be. There was little discrepancy between the 'is' and the 'ought', and therefore there was no need for a general explanation, hence the low level of curiosity about the children's backgrounds.

The typifications of individual children were, as elsewhere, sometimes explicitly associated with the 'family–home background theory', when work progress, behaviour or relations with other children were not acceptably explained as 'natural' or due to ill-health. One boy's poor behaviour was explained to me as a consequence of his being neglected by his father who had become preoccupied with yoga and meditation. But a 'family–home background theory' to explain 'children in this school' was only implied in the talk of teachers.

Virtually all the children wore what Miss Fox called 'school clothing'; most teachers used this term with amused reservation, and referred to 'school uniform'. The wearing of school uniform was interpreted as showing that the parents were cooperative and caring. One teacher suggested that some of them must find buying it a financial strain because they were owner occupiers with mortgages to pay.

Most of the girls wore 'sensible' and not 'fancy' shoes as at Seaton Park. For P.E. the girls wore white T shirts and their school uniform blue or maroon knickers; the boys a white T shirt and blue shorts; both wore black pull-on plimsolls. Mrs Silver commented on the appearance of the children compared with those at Burnley Road.

> 'I especially noticed that the 5-year-olds at Langley are very big and very healthy looking, plump and things. Whereas our 5-year-olds on the whole are terribly small and often very thin, and it was noticeable with the older children but not as marked.
> . . . our children have no uniform. I've had two children this term who didn't come to school because they didn't have any shoes to wear. The school welfare officer had to take them into town and buy shoes for them, which I imagine wouldn't happen at Langley.'

The connection between some of the favourable qualities of children and their homes made by the teachers, was one of association rather then explanation. Thus every reception class had some children who read, 'really read, not parrot fashion', before they came to school; a sign of interested and knowledgeable parents. One such infant reader knew no sounds. Her mother tackled her teacher: 'Someone's been teaching her phonetics.' Teachers reported that nearly all the parents turned up for Open Day meetings: a further index of general interest. When mixed-age classes were introduced just before my period of observation, many parents expressed concern that the older ones would be 'held back'. Miss Fox held a special meeting to justify the decision and to assuage their fears. Parental interest was also demonstrated for the teachers by the good response they had when they asked children to bring things from home. The books, toys, and games that the children brought in were generally approved by the teachers. One mother sent a 'present' of a Lego collection her children had grown out of, another indication of the continuity between home and school life. One teacher explained that the 'good coordination' of the reception children as due to their having done crayoning and painting at home. The children knew the traditional rhymes and stories before they started school, and some reported at news time that their parents read to them at bedtime. Mrs Silver commented on the parents:

> 'I saw them arriving in the morning by car which we [Burnley Road] don't get. We don't get any, I mean perhaps two out of the whole school come in by car. And they were driving a lot of them were driving to school and the children were coming out with flowers and things we don't get either, for the teachers.'

A further indication of the continuity between home and school was shown in parent helpers in the classroom; specifically this was a case of continuity between mothers and teachers. Mother-helpers looked like teachers, not surprisingly because some were teacher trained. They helped children with their practical mathematics and craft projects, supervised their play and read stories, often in an authentic teacher voice. Unlike Seaton Park and Burnley Road, Langley had a P.T.A. with a programme of well-attended meetings and a Ph.D. father as chairman. Virtually all the children took part in Sports Day which was confidently held on a Saturday; another indicator of parental interest and cooperation.

Unlike those at Seaton Park the teachers at Langley did not demonstrate a detailed knowledge of the locality, although two had lived in the area in the past. Their remarks were highly generalized: 'We have a very good area here', 'Just normal homes'. Although classroom activities provided teachers with some details of the children's homes, for example a histogram showing the distribution of terraced, semi-detached, and detached houses (ratio, 17, 12, 3), the children's home backgrounds were viewed as relatively homogeneous. Some children had local accents, others had 'educated' ones, but this seemed to have no significance for the teachers, some of whom had local accents themselves.

Only a few teachers compared the children and their home backgrounds to others in their experience. Six had been on the staff for a number of years and six others had not taught in any other school, which may form a partial explanation. It is possible that comparisons are made more often when the definition of the children requires explanation. The mothers among them did compare the children in the school favourably with their own, and talked about their own children in the classroom, something much less common in the other schools. One teacher had her own two children in the school and another's had been pupils there.

On several occasions Miss Fox was insistent that the school was not without its 'problems' and twice recounted how a boy had tried to extort money from others in the playground by threatening to cut their faces with a piece of slate he had in his pocket. David Hartley was told the same story for the same purpose of making token reservations about the children's otherwise favourable image.

The consequences of holding the definition?

At Burnley Road and Seaton Park I was able to identify some of the consequences of the teachers' definitions of 'most children' in those two schools—consequences which were consciously enacted and acknowledged by the teachers. But I was unable to do this in any satisfactory way at the Langley school. One reason for this is consistent with the theory I have posed. The definitions of the children at the other two schools were at variance with the definition of children made by the teachers' child-centred ideologies. The consequent actions on the part of the teachers were attempts to reduce that variance, to make the children of their experience correspond more closely to the children of their ideology, to bring the 'is' and the 'ought' together. At Langley the children were broadly defined as being as children ought to be: 'ordinary children', 'normal children'. Therefore, no special conscious actions were necessary; the children of their experience and their ideology were nearly identical.

A second reason concerns the headmistress, Miss Fox. It was very clear that many of the actions and policies of Mrs Brown at Burnley Road, and, to a lesser extent, Mrs Baker of Seaton Park, were consequences of the definition of the children and, more particularly, the related definition of their parents. Miss Fox's policy in relation to parents was consistent with their being defined as interested, informed and ambitious for their children. It was to meet their expectations, as she perceived them, of good progress in work and good levels of behaviour. This policy had two sets of related consequences, for the teachers and perhaps the children in the classroom, and for 'home–school' relations.

'Home–school' relations were fostered through a number of activities which were at least in part intended to show the parents that their children were successful and well behaved in school. In addition to the usual Nativity Play there was a hand-picked school choir and recorder consort which performed for parents and competed successfully in local competitions. On Sports Day all of the oldest age group gave a faultless display of country dancing, the result of months of practice, and a masterpiece of social control. At Burnley Road the children's craft products were put on public display; at Langley the children themselves were confidently displayed.

These activities were also partly intended to make sure of a continued supply of interested and ambitious parents. I have already mentioned how Langley attracted parents from outside the formal catchment area. These elements of parental choice were extended under the Nossex educational administration and Miss Fox was gratified to find more parents from outside the area 'coming to put their children's names down at the age of 3', attracted by the reputation of the school and the school uniform.

These parent-orientated activities had consequences for the teachers and children in terms of preparation and practice, but no more than at the other schools. More importantly, Miss Fox's relations with her staff may have been partly a consequence of her policy of pleasing parents. I am being deliberately tentative about this 'analysis' because it is based mainly on inference rather than any explication by the headmistress. Miss Fox attempted to exercise a tighter control on the activities of her teachers than either Mrs Brown or Mrs Baker. Mrs Silver made the comparison with Burnley Road.

'I wouldn't like to teach with the headmistress that was so directive, but I would say it was a lot easier to teach there . . . if you were willing to step down and be directed from above.'

Mrs Lamb made her comparisons

'After teaching at Seaton Park I felt rather constrained, but now we understand each other I feel I can do whatever I want to within reason, yes, provided the children are controlled, you know.'

Mrs Lamb's feelings of constraint were felt by other teachers, particularly those new to the staff. I was not able to discuss teacher–headteacher relationships at the group meetings because I felt constrained by the presence of Miss Fox, and so my evidence is from individual teachers. They referred to her expectations of high levels of success and standards of behaviour. They were urged to 'stretch' the children. They used a great deal of headmistress reference control with the children ('Now you know Miss Fox doesn't like you to be noisy.') They knew that the levels of attainment were compared across classes as a measure of teacher success. They even endured censure from Miss Fox in front of the children.

Miss Fox comes in and loudly rebukes Miss Fish for not returning some maths apparatus to the resource base. Miss Fish apologizes and explains it is being used continuously. Miss Fox says it must go back every day. She walks around the room inspecting the children's work and asking them questions, then addresses them. 'Children, please remember to return apparatus to the maths room.' At breaktime Miss Fish recounts the episode to the others. They commiserate and say similar things have happened to them.

Miss Fox justified this kind of thing as 'keeping up high standards'. A consequence was that some teachers were mildly anxious about her judgements. It is also possible that this had the consequence of making some of the children mildly anxious. The teachers were agreed that some children were rather anxious, they were 'anxious to please' and 'anxious to do well'; such phrases were applied to 8 per cent of the children in the records. There were certain kinds of behaviour which I only observed at the Langley school. When children got their work wrong or could not answer a question they often put on an embarrassed smile; when a mistake was made public other children sometimes laughed. At Burnley Road and Seaton Park children laughed at others' naughty behaviour. The teachers of older children at Langley were concerned that children helping one another did not turn into 'cheating'—a word never used in the other schools.

At the group meeting the teachers refuted my tentative suggestion that they may have anything to do with these mild anxieties of the children. They suggested these were due to parental pressure. Privately and individually some agreed with me, and reported that parents had accused 'the school' of putting too much pressure on the children. Their public refutation may have been partly due to my necessary omission of Miss Fox's part in generating their own mild anxiety.

In addition I suggested that their own anxiety may have had another origin. Having defined the children as being able and well behaved from supportive homes, any failure in work or behaviour would therefore reflect on their performance as teachers since there was no one else to blame. Those who spoke disagreed and some made the claim that the children did well and were well behaved because of their methods. Mrs Lamb, however, did agree with me, and in privately recalling her experience of Seaton Park said,

'The teachers in this school don't know how lucky they are with the kind of children they have to teach.'

This shifting explanation of the children's work and behaviour was very common: on the one hand their good qualities were the 'normal' products of 'normal homes', but on the other they were the outcome of 'good' teaching. Miss Fox's preference was for the latter explanation, particularly her part in 'keeping up standards'. However, some of her actions in relation to the recruitment of new children were consistent with the former. When the Nossex authority encouraged the headmistresses of first schools to take an interest in the playgroups in their areas Miss Fox visited a number outside her area, which was interpreted by some of her fellow heads as poaching for good parents as part of her recruitment campaign.

I prefaced this section by stating I was unable to show in any satisfactory way the direct consequences of the teachers' definition of the children and their parents at Langley school. Unlike those at Seaton Park or Burnley Road the teachers did not acceptably confirm my analysis, although it was presented only tentatively and incompletely. This unsatisfactory outcome will be returned to later in Chapter 14.

Permitted eccentric children from professional homes

In my observations I thought I detected the incidence of a special type of child in the life of the classroom, perhaps one or two in some classes, none in others. They had educated voices and seemed to be permitted a special status by the teacher. They appeared to attract and get a lot of her attention. One boy came to school for several days in a kilt. It was not his, he was not even Scottish, he had borrowed it from a neighbour. He was allowed to show it and himself off all round the school. Such children were excused playtime when they pathetically claimed a headache. One girl brought a note from her father asking for her to be excused from taking part in Sports Day 'because she feels she would rather not take part'. 'Strange child—her father's a psychologist,' said the teacher by way of explanation. Casually, it seemed that these children had professional fathers.

I put the idea of these permitted eccentric children from professional homes to the meeting of teachers and to my delight they recognized their existence. They were clever, 'sensitive' children, often with special talents, although a bit odd in their behaviour. This was part of their self-confidence. One teacher suggested, 'They do not have to conform like the lower middle class.'

This discussion had a most unexpected and unintended consequence, for although the teachers affectionately tolerated these children, they did not like their parents.

'They think no infant teacher has any intelligence.'

'They look down their noses at us.'

'They think it doesn't matter if the children are away for a day here or there, they can learn as much at home.'

'They don't really want to let their children come here. They think this is just a prelude to real education.'

The teachers were hurt by the rudeness of these professional parents, but more by the way their expertise and underlying ideology had been apparently scorned. The experience of being a social inferior was not a pleasant one.

The assessment of children

I have already reported in Chapter 8 that the teachers at the Langley school gave more favourable assessments to girls than boys. The well-kept records at the school enabled me to classify most of the children's social class backgrounds by their fathers' occupations. Table 11 shows that the 16 individual teachers assessing the children in their school class assessed girls more favourably than boys from the same social class background, assessed middle-class girls slightly more favourably than working-class girls, and assessed middle-class boys with markedly more favour than working-class boys.

Table 11 Teachers' ratings of the 'conduct' and 'attitude to work' of children in their school class ($n = 16$)

	Girls rated more favourably than boys		Middle class rated more favourably than working class	
	Middle class	Working class	Girls	Boys
'Conduct'	15	13	9	12
'Attitude to work'	11	15	10(1)	12

Note: (1) One teacher rated middle-class and working-class girls equally.

This pattern was also created from the data at Seaton Park, and was possibly associated with the dual definitions of 'most children' and 'nice children', and of 'most homes' and 'good homes'. 'Nice children' and 'good homes' were on the basis of assessments more commonly associated with middle-class and owner-occupied backgrounds. At Langley the teachers held unitary definitions of the children 'in this school' and of their home backgrounds. They were virtually all from owner-occupied housing, and with the exception of the handful of eccentric children from professional homes, the teachers gave no verbal indications of differentiating between children on the basis of any index of class, including father's occupation. But despite their different social awareness, the overal pattern of their assessments was similar to those of teachers at Seaton Park; middle-class girls received most favour and working-class boys least (compare Table 12 with Table 8). This pattern was also found in the mean reading quotients in the Young Test which was not based on the teachers' subjective assessments: middle-class girls 107.8, middle-class boys 102.2, working-class girls 101.5, working-class boys 95.8.

In discussing the pattern of teachers' assessments for Seaton Park I suggested that it was not the case that the teachers there regarded council house children or working-class children less favourably because they knew them to come from such backgrounds, but used their knowledge of the background to explain a poor

Table 12 Teachers' ratings of children's 'conduct' and 'attitude to work' (Percentages)

	(*n*)	'Conduct'		'Attitude to work'	
		Favourable	Unfavourable	Favourable	Unfavourable
Middle-class girls	(95)	68.4	3.2	64.2	3.2
Middle-class boys	(123)	39.8	20.3	47.2	21.1
Working-class girls	(93)	64.5	20.4	58.1	12.9
Working-class boys	(104)	30.8	25.0	37.5	35.6
All girls	(188)	66.5	11.7	61.2	8.0
All boys	(227)	35.7	22.4	42.7	27.8
All middle class	(218)	52.3	12.8	54.6	13.3
All working class	(197)	46.7	22.8	47.2	24.9

assessment. The recurrence of the pattern at Langley supports this, since the teachers there expressed virtually no recognition of differences in the children's social origins, and therefore could not have taken them into account in their assessments. In all three schools the teachers assessed and typified children on the basis of day-to-day activities in the classroom. The pattern of assessment at Langley and Seaton Park suggests that in the classroom situation created by infants' teachers, middle-class children tended to behave in ways closer to the teachers' definition of how children should behave, in accord with their child-centred ideology.

This suggestion requires an immediate modification. Girls seem to be closer to the definition of how children should be, than boys from the same social background. Table 11 shows that at Langley individual teachers' assessments showed more favour on the basis of sex than social class. This is also shown in the overall assessments in Table 12. Perhaps this is not surprising since at the Langley school (as in all schools) sex differences between pupils were highly visible, in that a teacher could see that a child being well or badly behaved was a boy or a girl, but differences in social background were relatively invisible. However, an inspection of Table 8 shows that at Seaton Park, too, the difference in assessments between the sexes was higher than that between social backgrounds, even where the teachers had some consciousness of the latter. These results have an important bearing on the discussion of the social nature of infant education to be made in the last two chapters.

CHAPTER FOURTEEN

Some Sociological Aspects of the Education of Infants

As with the report of any research based primarily upon observations this book is mainly descriptive. I have tried to give these descriptions some order and meaning using simple analyses, which lead to sets of explanations constituting a theory. I do not propose to give a summary of these observations, the analyses, and the theory. The main purpose of these last two chapters is to consider the nature of infant education as presented in the previous chapters, through two perspectives, the sociological and the educational. These are not completely discrete and some indications will be made of the ways they are related.

One of the reasons why I was attracted to research in infants' schools was that there had been little sociological interest in this sector of education. Since then the interest has grown resulting in a number of studies, the most significant being an essay by Basil Bernstein, 'Class and pedagogies. Visible and invisible' (1975), and the book by Rachel Sharpe and Antony Green, *Education and Social Control: a Study in Progressive Primary Education* (1975). I do not intend to give detailed summaries of these, or to make extended critiques. Instead I will comment on them in the light of my own studies, mainly to contrast our different approaches and theories.

The 'invisible pedagogy'?

Bernstein's essay is, to date, the latest in a series concerned with the sociology of the school and educational knowledge. I have already pointed out that, unlike his better-known work on language, these essays are not based upon original research and make few references to published research studies (King, 1976b). It follows that the essay in question must be somewhat speculative, although Bernstein's research on language has included studies of infants and their teachers, particularly that reported in Brandis and Bernstein (1974).

Bernstein's usual mode of analysis is through the creation of dichotomous typologies or dialectically related pairs of concepts. These include elaborated and restricted speech codes, positional and personal control, and collection and integrated knowledge codes. The latest addition is in the title of the paper: visible and invisible pedagogies. He proposes that in the pre-school and infants' school the pedagogy is invisible. Some of its characteristics are matched by my observations. 'Implicit' control corresponds to my oblique control (Chapter 6). The 'multiple and diffuse' criteria of evaluation are partly explicated in my analysis of the process of typifying individual children (Chapter 7).

Bernstein's terminology often has an attractive resonance, but it is difficult to conceive of an invisible pedagogy. Teachers' classroom control was clearly visible to the children (Chapter 6). The invisible qualities refer to what I have called the private elements of typification and assessment which are not revealed to the child, because they were defined as natural and developmental, and, in my explanation, because the teachers defined the child as innocent of responsibility for them (Chapter 7). What is missing from Bernstein's analysis is a consideration of the way in which the concept of development has consequences in the teachers' actions which tend to lead to the concept being sustained, as in their organization of reading, writing, and number work and their mediation of painting, drawing, and creative work (Chapters 1–5).

Social class differences in educational attainment have been the major theme of the sociology of education in this country, and the under-achievement of working-class children has been documented many times. In the two schools with mixed social compositions this was shown in the mean reading ages, as well as in teachers' subjective assessments of behaviour and progress (Chapters 12 and 13). In Bernstein's analysis of the infants' school this is explained by the origins of the invisible pedagogy with a new 'fraction' of the middle class. From this it follows that educational competence requires the use of his postulated elaborated speech code, which working-class children are supposed to have only a limited access to; hence their relative failure.

A number of reservations should be made about this thesis. The nature of this new middle class is only sketched by Bernstein, and he gives no indication as to how the basis of the proposed invisible pedagogy is transmitted from this class to the teachers. In Chapter 8 I suggested that infants' teachers encounter and accept child-centred ideologies as part of their professional socialization in colleges of education. The institutionalization of these ideologies as expressing the reality of children and their learning has been traced by Nanette Whitbread (1972). Whilst it is possible to regard such pioneers as Susan Isaacs as part of a new middle-class movement, her Chelsea Open Air Nursery School was ironically dubbed to be for 'Kensington cripples'; others, including Rachel and Margaret McMillan, dealt with working-class slum children. In addition, Phillippe Ariès (1962) has traced the origins of the social concept of childhood that underlies child-centredness to a period before the emergence of the class system of industrial society.

Bernstein suggests that the middle-class mother provides a 'model' for the infants' teacher, but does not explain how this occurs. The teachers in my study did not consciously model themselves on middle-class mothers, although some of them were, incidentally, middle-class mothers. Teachers at Seaton Park school tended to show greater approval of middle-class homes and so implicitly the mothers, and at Burnley Road there was explicit disapproval of some working-class mothers (Chapter 12 and 10).

Social class differences in education have received much attention, but, as I have pointed out before (1971), sex differences in education have been largely ignored by sociologists (the work of David Hartley mentioned in Chapter 7 should help to remedy this). In all three schools girls had higher reading ages and had more favourable teacher assessments than boys, and at Seaton Park and Langley these sex differences were found within social classes, and were arguably bigger than the class differences. Perhaps Bernstein's suggestion that middle-class mothers form the model for infants' teachers could be seen as an explanation of middle-class girls receiving the most favourable assessments and working-class boys the least? Two reservations should be made about this. Firstly, the longitudinal study of families in Nottingham by the husband and wife team of John and Elizabeth Newson (1976) showed that middle-class mothers differentiated less between their sons and daughters than did working-class mothers.

The second reservation concerns the sex of the teachers. Whilst some of their activities show convergence with those of mothers and housewives, Mr Green, whom I described in Chapter 8, was a typical infants' teacher. I mentioned in Chapter 8 that the change from infants' school to first school was associated with the appointment of more men. An inspection of their assessments show that they showed much the same level of favour towards girls as did their women colleagues.

Bernstein's essay illustrates the limitations of speculative analysis as a form of theorizing isolated from empirical research. As with his other work in this field his attractive terminology has only limited usefulness, but may gain acceptance because of his undoubted eminence in the sociology of education.

'Education and social control'

Unlike Bernstein's essay, Sharp and Green's book is a research study of a single school in a working-class area. Observations, by three observers using different methods of observation, were carried out in a small number of classrooms, but the study was primarily based upon tape-recordings of interviews with the headteacher and three teachers giving accounts of their aims and classroom activities. The authors started out using a phenomenological perspective, which was the main element in the 'new' sociology referred to in the Introduction. Just as the phenomenological philosophy it is partly derived from emphasizes 'the thing in itself', so social phenomenology emphasizes the situation in itself. Thus the social situation of the everyday life of the classroom must be explained in terms of the social elements of which it is immediately comprised. During the research Sharp and Green began to concur with the criticisms that have been made of social phenomenology. In emphasizing the importance of men as the creators of social structure, it tends to ignore the constraint this structure imposes on men's actions. At the extreme the sanctity of the situation leads to a neglect of events in the past and those external to the situation.

Sharp and Green's response to this was to introduce a marxist element to 'correct' the perspective. They do not use the crudest form of economic or materialistic determinism that marxist theory can take, in which the economic infrastructure of ownership and the means of production in a capitalist society determines the social and cultural superstructure, including education. But their conclusions about progressive education do stress the importance of social and economic structures external to the classroom situation: the antithesis of the phenomenological approach. Briefly, they conclude that classroom activities, including social control and the assessment of progress, contribute to the conservation of the existing social order, and on this account child-centred education is judged to have failed.

Sharp and Green make suitable reservations about the exploratory nature of their study and its limited range. Other reservations may be made. Although observations were made in three classrooms most of the evidence consists of the interviews referred to already, and the judgements of the child-centred approach are based more upon the accounts teachers gave of what they did and why they did it, than upon what they were observed to do. The best-known piece of phenomenological research in the sociological of education is that of Nell Keddie (1971), in which she showed the disparity between what she calls the educationalist and teacher contexts; that is, between what teachers say about teaching among themselves, and their actions in the classroom. Sharp and Green's 'probing' interviews constitute what might be called the research context, and may also be remotely related to the teacher context. My approach was to observe the classroom activities and talk to the teacher afterwards about what we had both seen.

Teachers' assessments of children's work progress are seen by Sharp and Green as an early stage of the processes of selection and allocation to the occupational structure. Talcott Parsons (1961) made a similar analysis of the American elementary school classroom from the functionalist viewpoint, which stresses the dependent relationship of education to the rest of society; an approach which Sharp and Green criticize. They confine their analysis to an examination of the three teachers' typifications of small number of children. On the basis of my analysis of the teachers' assessments of several hundred children in three schools, girls, as a group, were found to be the more favourably assessed. How does this early sex differentiation relate to eventual occupational placement where women are disfavoured in opportunities? The long-term outcomes of the educational process are not a sufficient explanation of that process, whether the theory is functionalist or marxist. Neither encompasses the complexities of classroom activities, and both reduce the humanity of teachers and children. There is little to choose between being the 'cultural dope' of functionalism or suffering from the 'false consciousness' of marxism.

Sharp and Green's conclusions do not arise directly from the limited research evidence they present, but are corollaries of the marxist perspective they adopt. In essence their conclusions would apply to almost any modern educational process, and so leave largely out of account anything that is particular to infant education, including the teachers' beliefs and meanings.

Weberian action theory

I do not propose to make a detailed exposition of my theoretical approach. As far as this study is concerned it has been expressed throughout the reporting of the research, and cannot be easily separated from it. In the Introduction I called it action theory of a fairly simple kind, and acknowledged Weber's definition of social action as my starting-point. Although I have used some of the ideas of Schutz I have not followed a phenomenological approach. I do not accept that social situations are explicable without reference to external factors, and agree with the criticism that phenomenology tends to be ahistorical and ignores the constraints of social structure. However, I do not accept the functionalist view of education as being adaptive to the 'needs' of society, or the marxist view of it as 'an ideological illusion'.

For Weber functionalism was a second best (1922, 1968), and in his 'debate with the ghost of Marx' he modified marxist economic determinism by stressing the importance of ideas in social life, principally through his study, *The Protestant Ethic and the Spirit of Capitalism* (1904, 1930). In this study I have stressed the way in which the institutionalized ideologies of infant education inform the actions of teachers in the classroom. These ideologies are human products with historical locations, transmitted by established agencies, including colleges, books, and other expert opinion.

The 88 000 infants' teachers in this country constitute a social group which has class characteristics, in Weber's (1948) use of the term, in that they occupy a particular position in the economic order in terms of remuneration and conditions of work. But they are also a status group, again in Weber's usage, with shared perspectives and social identities, and a particular social position, which is certainly related to their being mainly women, more than 99 per cent nationally. Their institutionalized ideologies are better regarded as part of their status culture rather than being a simple derivative of their economic class. Other teachers occupy a similar class position but do not accept all aspects of the child-centred ideology. These certainly include the deviant teachers described in Chapter 8, and many junior school teachers interviewed in the general survey. (Teachers of young children in the U.S.A. presumably hold much the same position in the economic order as their British counterparts, but the admiration and advocacy of British primary education by Americans such as Silberman (1970) indicates that they do not necessarily hold the same ideologies or follow the same practices.) The ideological dissent between infants' and junior school teachers, mentioned in Chapter 1, may be seen as confirming Weber's conflict model of society, in which groups compete for the maintenance or improvement of their economic, power or, in this case, status positions.

However, not all of the infants' teachers' actions were informed by their status group ideologies. Sometimes they were more related to their economic and social positions as lower middle-class salary earners, and as wives and mothers, as shown in some of their orientations towards parents, especially at the Seaton Park and Burnley Road schools (Chapters 10 and 12).

Unlike Marx and Durkheim (the inspiration of Bernstein and much of functionalism), Weber did not construct models of the nature of society. Instead he provided ways of exploring and explaining its nature, which admit its fundamental duality in being constructed and maintained by the actions of men, but also in constraining their actions. The ideologies of infant education are human products, the acceptance of which constrained teachers and through them the children they taught. The study of educational ideologies enables connections to be made between social life at the small-scale level of the classroom and school, with historical events and with large-scale elements of the general social structure; exercises in what C. Wright Mills (1959) called 'the sociological imagination'.

Grounded theory

I mentioned in the Introduction that I initially tried to follow some of the ideas of Glaser and Strauss (1968). The experience of this research leads me to have several reseverations about grounded theory. My theory is not totally grounded on data; its essential form was based upon my adopting an action approach. In proposing that theory can be 'discovered' from data, Glaser and Strauss ignore the way in which the act of research actually creates the data. However, I did use the method of comparative analysis they advocate, in delineating the ideal typical infants' teacher by comparison with deviant teachers (Chapter 8), and in posing the theory of teachers' typifications of children by comparing these across the three schools (Chapters 11, 12, and 13). I also followed them in putting my theories to the teachers I studied. (This is Schutz's 'postulate of adequacy' (1953). Curiously, Glaser and Strauss make no reference to Schutz in their book.) However, my experience at the Langley school, when some of my admittedly tentative explanations were not supported by some of the teachers (Chapter 13), lead me to question its general applicability. John Rex (1973) has defined a sociologist as an observer 'with the capacity to make observations of social reality distinct from those of the participant actors'. By the time I went to the Langley school I had made observations of the social realities of the teachers at Burnley Road and Seaton Park, and I used these observations in my interpretation of the social reality of the teachers at Langley, but, with the exception of Mrs Lamb, they had no experience of these other realities. A starting-point of my research was to pose the reality of the classroom as problematic, as something to be explained. At Seaton Park and particularly Burnley Road the teachers also had a reality problem, in that the definition based upon their ideologies of how the children should be was at variance with how the children 'were', and they attempted to solve this problem by posing the 'family–home background theory' (Chapters 10, 11, and 12). They accepted my analysis of their problems and my theory of their 'theory', because there was no fundamental contradiction involved. The teachers at the Langley school did not have this problem of the discrepancy between what the children 'were' and what they ought to be. But when I suggested that this may be explained in terms of the children's backgrounds some refuted it and claimed the fit was due to their good teaching. I fear that sociologists will always be faced with the situation described by Merton (1959). If they confirm conventional wisdom they are judged to have wasted their time by proving the obvious. If they deny conventional wisdom, they are not believed.

Self-fulfilling prophecies?

Throughout the book I have used W. I. Thomas's definition of the situation as a theoretical touchstone. 'If men define situations as real they are real in their consequences.' In several ways this is a neat summary of Weber's views of the nature of social action (Chapter 2), and Aaron Cicourel (1964) considers it to express much of Schutz's views about social life, not surprisingly since Weber's ideas form one of the starting-points of Schutz's. It also forms the basis of Robert Merton's (1968) self-fulfilling prophecy. 'The self-fulfilling prophecy is, in the beginning, a *false* definition of the situation evoking new behaviour which makes the originally false conception come *true*.'

It has been fashionable to pose the existence of self-fulfilling prophecies in education. This has been called the 'Pygmalion effect' after the ethically dubious experiment in America by Rosenthal and Jacobson (1968), who let teachers have the names of children randomly designated as about to bloom or spurt intellectually. Rosenthal and Jacobson reported that some of these children did improve their intelligence scores, and claim that these gains were the outcome of a self-fulfilling prophecy. However, these results have been disputed, and replications of the experiment have produced different results. In the slightly more acceptable study by Rist (1970) he claims that the self-fulfilling prophecy accounts for the failure of the poorest children in the black ghettos. These and other studies have lead to the proposition, made, for example, by Estelle Fuchs (1973), that working-class failure in general is the outcome of such a prophecy, in these terms: teachers' falsely define working-class children as being less able and this evokes new behaviour which leads to the children doing less well in school than they might.

Was such a self-fulfilling prophecy at work in the schools I studied? With minor reservations I will make later, I could find no evidence for this. At Burnley Road the teachers recognized (indirectly) the children as being working class, and defined them as being below average for progress (Chapter 10). However, the manifest and purposeful consequences of this definition were attempts to improve their levels of progress through remedial reading, speech therapy, and the adjustment class (Chapter 11). (Their efforts may have been successful—see Chapter 15.) In all three schools, 'poor' progress or behaviour of some individual children was subsequently explained in terms of the teachers' family–home background theory (Chapter 7). This is in reverse of the requirements of a self-fulfilling prophecy, where the social background information should precede the definition and consequent progress and behaviour.

At Seaton Park the teachers' definition of 'nice children' from 'good homes' did show some, but not complete, coincidence with middle-class children from owner-occupied housing, but once again home background information was sought to explain lack of progress and did not precede it (Chapter 12). At the Langley school the teachers made no distinction between children of different social classes (other than the handful of permitted eccentrics from professional homes), but the social class pattern of their assessments was similar to that found at Seaton Park, so that the 'consequence' of working-class lower favourableness could not have followed the teachers falsely defining working-class children as less able (Chapter 13). This also applies to the lower mean reading ages of working-class children in all three schools, since the test was the same for all children and was not set by the teachers.

In Rist's study he assumed a correlation between the colour and social status of the children: the darker the lower. Social status was therefore visible. The low status of children at Burnley Road was visible to the teachers but they were not held responsible for their clothing and cleanliness by their teachers, and I could detect no evidence of a 'halo effect' whereby favourable appearance was used to indicate other favourable qualities (Chapter 10). Appearance could, however, be used as an indirect explanation of poor work and behaviour. One characteristic of all children was highly visible, that of their sex (Chapter 7). A social class self-fulfilling prophecy would not account for the more favourable ratings and higher reading ages of girls compared with boys from similar backgrounds. Explanations of social class differences in education that ignore sex differences are as unacceptable as explanations of sex differences which ignore social class.

My minor reservations both concern Burnley Road. Out of their classroom experience the teachers defined the children as lacking in useful experiences and knowledge. On one occasion I observed that this was a false definition which was made 'true' by the teacher's actions.

The class of 7-year-olds had been watching a television programme on castles. In the follow-up discussion the teacher asked who had visited a castle. Several said they had, and referred to a 'tower thing', 'in a park', 'in the town'. The teacher tried to identify this as a well-known castle outside Newbridge but the children insisted it was in the town. 'No, you must be making a mistake.' In fact, the tower remains of Newbridge castle are in a park in the town centre. In this single observed example the teacher's ignorance sustained a false definition of the children's ignorance.

Burnley Road was an infants' school during the main period of my observations, but I returned there several times later when it was a first school. At Seaton Park and Langley, children in the top age group practised joined writing, but at Burnley Road they did not, because 'well, they are just not up to it yet'. Children defined as not being up to doing joined writing were not taught joined writing, and so were not allowed to demonstrate whether they could do joined writing. This is the definition of the situation in operation. There was no way that the teachers or anyone else could know if the definition of the children's capacity was a false one.

This also serves to contrast the definition of the situation with the self-fulfilling prophecy. The former poses a relativist view of reality in which what is 'real' is defined, acted upon, and sustained in the situation. In dealing with 'false' definitions the latter poses the existence of 'real' ones—an absolutist notion of reality. The idea of self-fulfilling prophecies in education is an attractive one to some people in that it puts the blame for failure on the teacher and not the child. But if a child's ability has been falsely defined, how is his 'real' ability to be discovered? Merton's transformation of Thomas's definition of the situation into the self-fulfilling prophecy therefore involved a major theoretical change, but one of doubtful usefulness in education.

The family socialization theory

How then are the variations in the performance and assessment of children to be explained? The teachers explained these firstly in terms of the individuality and the relative development of children, and to some extent the sex differences were accounted for in this way, but when these were not acceptable they posed either an illness or 'family–home background theory'.

The sociological version of the teachers' 'theory' is part of the orthodox explanation of social class differences in education. Briefly, it poses that children's school progress is associated with the differences in forms of child rearing and family life, which are well established to vary by social class. Much research has been directed towards investigating which elements of middle-class family socialization confer educational advantage, Bernstein's theory of language codes being perhaps the most sophisticated version. Those who propose the self-fulfilling prophecy do so against this kind of explanation, so shifting the 'blame' not only from the working-class children, but also from their families.

My research was not directly concerned with the children's homes or family lives and so I have little evidence with which to discuss this family socialization theory, but what little I have leads me to support it.

When mothers brought their children to Seaton Park for the first time, Mrs Baker asked them to fill in a questionnaire 'to help us in getting to know your child'. It consisted of 14 items each to be rated on a 5-point scale: always, usually, sometimes, seldom, never. Mrs Baker admitted that some mothers were confused by the task and others were a little worried by it, which was reflected in the number of spoilt and incomplete returns. The teachers reported they took little notice of the information, preferring as always to rely on their own experience of the child.

Table 13 shows the mothers' ratings analysed by the sex of the child and the social class based on fathers' occupations. The nature of the sample and the incompleteness of the data means that any interpretation must be very cautious, but a familiar pattern emerges. Mothers' ratings for the skills and competences of counting, dressing, going to the toilet, tying shoe-laces, and practising road safety were generally higher for girls in each social class. These assessments could have been made reasonably objectively by the mothers, but their reports of other attributes may reflect different expectations, standards, and opportunities for boys and girls, in different social class backgrounds. Helping, memory, self-amusement, playing happily with other children, and liking painting and modelling were all rated higher by middle-class mothers of children of both sexes.

Table 13 Mothers' ratings of children (percentages of 'always' or 'always' plus 'usually')

	Middle class		Working class	
	Girls	Boys	Girls	Boys
	% (n)	% (n)	% (n)	% (n)
Can count ten objects*	78.6 (28)	60.0 (25)	71.1 (38)	40.0 (25)
Dresses himself*	56.7 (30)	39.1 (23)	61.0 (41)	21.4 (28)
Goes to the toilet by himself*	93.3 (30)	76.0 (25)	95.0 (40)	86.2 (29)
Can tie shoe-laces †	36.8 (19)	29.2 (24)	34.2 (38)	19.2 (26)
Practises road safety drill †	59.3 (27)	65.2 (23)	62.9 (35)	55.5 (27)
Feeds himself*	86.2 (24)	100.0 (29)	89.2 (37)	92.3 (26)
Helps with activities in the home †	71.9 (32)	53.5 (22)	50.0 (40)	42.3 (26)
Shows interest in his surroundings*	51.7 (29)	64.0 (25)	63.4 (41)	37.5 (24)
Speaks clearly*	79.3 (29)	53.8 (26)	67.5 (40)	65.4 (26)
Talks freely to strangers †	60.0 (30)	44.0 (25)	51.2 (41)	63.0 (27)
Good memory for people and places*	57.6 (33)	60.0 (25)	47.5 (40)	53.9 (26)
Keeps himself amused*	46.7 (30)	47.8 (23)	39.0 (41)	42.3 (26)
Plays happily with other children*	71.9 (27)	53.5 (25)	50.0 (40)	42.3 (26)
Likes painting and modelling*	79.3 (29)	71.4 (21)	69.2 (39)	66.7 (24)

Notes: * Rated 'always'.
      † Rated 'always' or 'usually'.

Mrs Baker admitted that the 14 items represented qualities that were desirable in a child starting school, although she had reservations about tying shoe-laces (becoming rarer) and the possibility of different interpretations of 'talking freely to strangers'. On this basis high scores may be taken as being favourable in terms of the prognosis of classroom learning and behaviour. The familiar pattern is that of slightly greater favour towards middle-class children, especially girls, and somewhat less towards working-class children, especially boys. This was also seen in the teachers' ratings of children's behaviour and attitude to work, and in the mean reading quotients (Chapters 12 and 13). Furthermore, similar sex and social class variations were found in the much more secure and extensive work of the Newsons (1976) based upon interviews with mothers. They conclude that middle-class families are the more child-centred, and that among the working class child-centredness is higher for daughters. This suggests and advantageous fit between child-centred families and child-centred education.

I am not able to classify the parents who completed the questionnaire in terms of their child-centredness. However, there were statistically significant correlations between the mothers' reports of their children, evaluated as favourable in prognosis by the headmistress (and possibly the teachers), and the teachers' initial ratings of the children's 'conduct' and 'attitude to work'. A simple score for favourable prognosis for each child was obtained by the addition of the number of items his or her mother reported he or she 'always' did. An arbitrary score of three was given for a favourable assessment by the teacher for 'conduct' or 'attitude to work', two for a mixed or neutral assessment, and one for an unfavourable assessment. These assessments were made three to nine months after the mothers made their reports.

The product–moment correlation between favourable prognosis based upon mothers' reports of children's behaviour and teachers' assessments of 'conduct' was $0.914 (n = 113)$. That for assessment of 'attitude to work' was 0.912. (As may be expected, the correlation between teachers' assessments of 'conduct' and 'attitude to work' was also high at 0.956.)

I have made reservations about the raw data used in these calculations, and an arbitrary element of quantification was used. Also it must be pointed out that it was not possible to include data for all the children in the school. Even without these reservations the correlations would not 'prove' the family socialization theory to be correct, but even as they stand, they are at least consistent with it. They certainly support Mrs Baker's view that many of the qualities she listed in her questionnaire were favourable ones for the children's learning and behaviour.

Children spend the first five years of their lives before starting school in families where basic relationships between parents and children vary by social class and the sex of the child. Similar variations were found in the relationships the children enter into with the teachers when they go to school. I have expressed strong doubts about the possibility of the teachers being responsible for social class differences in attainment by the operation of a self-fulfilling prophecy. Such a proposition poses that children are totally powerless in the classroom situation and bring nothing of the rest of their social lives into it. But infants' teachers acting in accord with their child-centred ideologies created situations in which children could express and demonstrate knowledge, competences, and forms of behaviour which had origins outside the classroom. This was shown very clearly in talking, writing, drawing, painting, and playing activities, thought to express their interests and individuality (Chapters 3, 4, and 5).

The definition of the situation was only one element of W. I. Thomas's analysis of the total situation, which was completed by 'objective conditions' and 'pre-existing attitudes of individuals and groups'. In ignoring the latter some have equated the definition of the situation with the total situation. With respect to the classroom this means ignoring the 'pre-existing attitudes' of the teachers, in terms of their personal biographies, social backgrounds, professional education, and experiences, shown to be very important at Burnley Road (Chapter 10), and also those of the children in terms of their previous and continuing experiences outside of school, particularly in their families.

This discussion leaves unexamined the nature of infant education which leads to different outcomes for children of different sex and social class. I will attempt to do this in the final chapter in a discussion of the educational implications of the research.

CHAPTER FIFTEEN

The Nature of Infant Education

My research was concerned with describing, analysing, and explaining the activities occurring in infants' classrooms. When I started I explicitly denied to the teachers that I was an expert in this area of education. Having done the research I am now in the position of having observed more classrooms for longer stretches of time than most teachers, headteachers, and many of those who would claim to be experts. However, if I have now acquired some expertise it is in what happens in infant education and not in what should happen. There is no aspect of my research which in itself suggests what should be done in the education of young children. To move from the research concerned with what happened, to any discussion about what should happen involves the introduction of value-judgements.

I shall try to make any such judgements as explicit as possible in the discussion that follows. This will be in two related parts. The first accepts all the value-judgements implicit in the observed practices of infants' teachers, and leaves unexamined the child-centred ideology which informs them. This acceptance is not necessarily personal to me but was basic to the teachers, with the possible exception of the deviants described in Chapter 8. This first part will centre on teacher defined problems, particularly those at the Burnley Road school. The second part of the discussion will examine the nature of infant education, including the extent to which this may have contributed to these problems.

The problems at Burnley Road

I described in the Introduction my dissatisfaction with my previous experience of large-scale research. I found the refreshment I sought in doing this study, but I am left with a sense of responsibility towards the teachers I have described here, even though they are wrapped in pseudonymity and may never read what I have written about them. This particularly applies to the Burnley Road teachers. In writing about them I have felt a slight sense of betrayal, although nothing I have written has been intended as a criticism of them or any other teachers. After my meeting with them to discuss the research I wrote in my notebook, 'I wish I could have been more helpful, more constructive.' The following discussion concerns what might be done so that their dilemmas and problems, described in Chapters 10 and 11, might be reduced to the levels of satisfaction of the teachers at Seaton

Park or even the Langley school, without changing their basic practices or examining the underlying ideologies.

Parent–teacher relations

Teachers at Burnley Road and Seaton Park explained the levels of progress and standards of behaviour in terms of their 'family–home background theory'. If this theory is accepted to have some validity, and I suggested in the last chapter that it has, then it might be proposed that attempts may be made to alter the home circumstances and family lives of the children. Put in this bald way the political and moral problems involved are enormous, but efforts were made to do this through housing policy and the health and social welfare services. Health visitors, social workers, and others are constantly trying to change families according to models of what they think they should be like. This is a vast subject and so I will confine my comments to what those in schools may do.

Mrs Brown's policy was to get the parents 'on our side a bit', Mrs Baker's to mobilize their interest usefully. There is no way of knowing whether their policies had consequences for the childrens' behaviour and progress. The Plowden Committee believed that increasing parental interest would lead to improvements in their children's learning. This was based upon a spurious interpretation of survey results which assumed a causal connection between the two. Improving parent–teacher relations is probably better argued in terms of the parents' right to know about their children's education, and the teachers' responsibility to explain and justify it.

A different approach would be to change the population of parents. Several teachers at Burnley Road blamed their problems on the nature of the catchment area and thought it should be redrawn so that some of the children went to other schools. The educational geography of Newbridge would probably allow this, although there would be political problems, and the change would probably have to be accompanied by a reduction of parental choice of school to be effective. This would parallel the programmes of integration for immigrant children in this country and those for black children in the U.S.A.

An alternative would be to change the local housing policy of nearly half a century and stop concentrating 'bad tenants' and 'problem families' in the Burnley Road area. This would probably pose even more political problems.

Material provision

In defining the E.P.A. school the Plowden Committee recommended that it should receive extra money as part of a policy of positive discrimination. Burnley Road was designated a Social Priority School and received the financial benefits described in Chapter 9. Before this it was as well provided for as most schools in Newbridge, and was therefore not 'deprived' in this sense. Mrs Brown thought that the benefits were welcome but not very helpful.

I have concluded elsewhere that the existing differences in material provision probably do not have important consequences for the levels of attainment in different schools (1977), although the existing differences are relatively small. However, it is doubtful whether more books, tape-recorders or even bigger classrooms would alleviate the teachers' problems at Burnley Road, although these might be valued for other reasons.

Burnley Road received one extra teacher as a result of its S.P.S. designation. Significant consequences may have followed if the number of teachers had been doubled and so the size of classes halved, assuming twice the number of classrooms could be made available, or the total number of children in the school halved. The evidence concerning size of class and children's attainment contradicts conventional wisdom in that the research of Alan Little (1971) and many others found higher attainment in larger classes. But these studies were concerned with existing variations in size of class which are relatively small, certainly not including any of 15 children. At this size attainment may be improved; certainly the problems of control that teachers at Burnley Road faced would be eased. However, the cost of such a provision would be very high, teachers' wages being the largest part of any education budget.

Pre-school education

Teachers in the reception classes at Burnley Road said they had to resort to nursery education with their children. There was one nursery school in Newbridge, and 17.5 per cent of children at Burnley Road had been there. Several teachers remarked favourably about them. This was shown in their reading ages; they were 0.9 years below average in the Ladybird Series compared with the 1.1 years of other children. They were absent less often, 7.7 times a term compared with 12.3, and the boys among them received more favourable conduct comments from teachers, 77.2 per cent compared with 41.2 per cent.

These figures do not necessarily prove that nursery education had favourable consequences. (Nor does the general research, for example Woodhead (1976).) Mrs Brown did not know the basis upon which children were selected to attend nursery school and so it is not known how they compared with those not selected in terms of home background. But assuming they were similar it may be suggested that more nursery provision would be helpful, particularly in improving the boys' behaviour, a special problem at Burnley Road.

A number of pre-school playgroups existed in Newbridge. At the time I was at Burnley Road few children attended these, but under the Nossex authority they were encouraged and more children began to do so. At Seaton Park, 30.8 per cent of children had attended playgroups according to the school records, but there was no general feeling among the teachers there that there were strong advantages to this. This was shown in the analysis of the records where no significant differences in reading age or teachers' assessments were found between playgroup attenders and others, keeping sex and social class constant.

I have no first-hand knowledge of the playgroups, but all three headmistresses considered them widely variable in terms of preparing children for the reception class. It is possible that attendance of some form of playgroup could have favourable consequences for the children at Burnley Road. It is also possible that mothers' involvement in playgroups may have consequences for the way they relate to their own children.

Pre-school education may also be valued intrinsically, as providing worth-while experiences for children. The alternatives for some include playing in the street all day or being left with a child-minder.

Classroom practices

The suggestions made so far have not concerned what teachers do in the classroom. In Chapter 1, I suggested that the teachers, with the exception of the deviants described in Chapter 8, were secure in their acceptance of the child-centred ideology. This did not mean that they all used exactly the same classroom practices, and I have indicated some of the sources of variation in my descriptions. The account of the unfortunate Mrs White (Chapter 6) whose class was out of control indicates that teachers varied in their effectiveness, judged by their own criteria. But it is difficult to be clear about which practices are more effective. In Chapter 6 I suggested that teachers who were satisfied with the control they exercised over the children made their expectations clear and rewarded conformity with those expectations.

Some of the teachers at the Langley school wanted to claim that the good behaviour and progress of the children were outcomes of their classroom practices. Miss Fox, the headmistress, endorsed this view in claiming the effectiveness of her insistence on standards, although her actions in relation to recruitment showed her acceptance of the alternative explanation, the family–home background theory (Chapter 13).

Can the differences in the children's behaviour and progress found in the three schools be explained by differences in pedagogical practice? When Mrs Silver compared the Langley school with Burnley Road, and when, on the basis of actual teaching, Mrs Lamb compared it with Seaton Park, they concluded that the differences were attributable to the children. In my observations I found as much variation in classroom practice within the three schools as between them, although I must stress that the similarities between all the teachers were far more substantial than the differences. There was generally more freedom of movement allowed to the children at Seaton Park, made possible by the large classrooms, and this may have made their 'bounciness' more evident. The generally smaller classrooms of the Langley school constrained mobility. I have suggested that Miss Fox's insistence on standards may have had the consequence of making some of the teachers slightly anxious about meeting her expectations, but they did not accept my suggestion that they in turn generated slight anxieties in their 'anxious to please' children. In this they returned to the family–home background theory and cited pushing parents (Chapter 13).

The only satisfactory way to have investigated this would have been to have arranged for the Burnley Road children to have been taught by the teachers from the Langley school, or, in view of her claim that 'this school is what I have made it', for Miss Fox to have changed appointments with Mrs Brown at Burnley Road. Such experiments are unlikely to happen. What could be done is to try to find a school with a social composition similar to that of Burnley Road where the children's behaviour and progress are objectively 'better', and one with a similar social composition to the Langley school where they are 'worse'. A more feasible and equally interesting investigation would be to find a school where the mean reading age of the working-class pupils was higher than that of the middle-class pupils (and where the mean for the boys was higher than that for the girls). If such schools exist, then they could be investigated to see if the teachers' practices differ from those in other schools.

After I had finished writing this section Mrs Brown sent me the reading scores for Burnley Road from the Young Test for 1977. I was able to calculate for her that the mean quotient was 92.4, an increase of over 10 points from 1975 (Chapter 10), and one that was bigger for boys than girls. Boys had increased from 78.5 to 91.0 and girls from 86.9 to 93.4. These rises were probably not due to changes in the school population because as I reported in Chapter 9, the evidence was that the school population had if anything become less favourable in the headmistress's estimation. Mrs Brown was gratified by the increases and assured me that the children had not been practising the tests. Her explanation was that 'we have been putting a lot into the reading', using some of the methods described in Chapter 11. Perhaps the Plowden Committee was right in suggesting that what E.P.A. children required were mainly good, ordinary primary schools?

The nature of infant education

The discussion so far has been based upon an acceptance of the child-centred ideologies of infant education and the extent to which teacher-defined problems could be eased without questioning their practices and the legitimating ideologies. Can it be posed that these problems were the outcome of those practices? This question cannot be answered directly because I only observed existing practices. There is no way of knowing whether the problems would disappear if the practices were changed or whether new problems would be created. The only way to know would be to implement changes and observe the outcomes. What follows must be therefore rather speculative, and must pose many unanswered and, as yet, unanswerable questions.

In Chapter 1, I pointed out that the child-centred ideologies which represent what is 'real' about children and their learning to infants' teachers, are social constructs; there was a time when they did not exist and they are not accepted by everyone. Children have learnt and still learn, in some parts of the world, basic skills by methods far removed from those I have described. Within this perspective, classroom practices and ideologies may be discussed and evaluated independently of any claims for their being the best or the truth.

Play

Among the many purposes they attributed to play, the teachers emphasized 'play as learning' (Chapter 2). Children have learnt and do learn the three R's in other times and places without any play elements, so that this cannot be essential. Since all children did 'learning by playing' I have no adequate way of estimating its effectiveness in the three schools. The only easy judgement possible is whether it is desirable. Whether they learnt what their teachers thought they did or not, most children seemed happy when they played, and on this account alone it could be considered worthwhile, particularly at Burnley Road, especially if the teachers' ideas about the limited nature of their activities outside school were correct.

But does play get in the way of learning? Would the children at Burnley Road have mastered the basics better if they did them all day and never played? This idea was part of the pre-school intervention programme described by Bereiter and Engelmann (1966) in the U.S.A. English infants' teachers would find the old-fashioned didactic methods they used an affront to their child-centred ideologies, but of all the programmes tried, it seems one of the most effective in terms of improved test scores.

Classroom control

In Chapter 6, I suggested that a major element in the oblique forms of social control used by teachers was the idea that young children were innocent in their intentions, even if their behaviour was defined as naughty. There are two important considerations that follow from this practice, one theoretical and the other practical.

This particular view of innocence touches upon the relationship between man and society and the issue of free will. It is recognized that men make society but are also constrained by it (Chapter 13). The phenomenologists stress the first part of the relationship, the marxists and functionalists the latter. Weber tried to contain both in his sociology, in that, given the inseparable nature of man and society, it was still possible to pose that an individual may freely choose a course of action against societal constraints. At what point may children be regarded as being in this position? When may it be judged that a child has freely chosen to break the rules established by the powerful in the society of the classroom? I have suggested that the teachers' actions were such that the children tended to conform with the definitions that informed those actions, which were based upon child-centred ideologies. At Burnley Road the definition of innocence was difficult for the teachers to sustain (Chapter 11). Would their dilemmas about the children's behaviour have been eased or solved if they had interpreted naughty behaviour as an outcome of the children's free choice, that they intended or chose to be naughty? Would the occasional pinching, punching, and pushing have stopped if they had not ignored it?

The forms of child behaviour approved by the teachers included being quiet, busy, tidy, helpful, kind, and conventionally polite, and much of their control was directed towards promoting them. Are these desirable qualities in a child, or should they be changed?

Children's interests

Many classroom activities were based upon teachers' imputations of children's interests, but in Chapter 4 I described how interests could be induced and others ignored by the teacher. Should the children's 'true' interests have been completely acknowledged and incorporated into the educational process as part of the idea of child-centredness? At Burnley Road this would have meant a curriculum for the boys which legitimated their manifest interest in fighting, wars, and violence in general, an interest which posed a problem for the teachers because it contradicted the definition of the children as innocent.

Given that many interests were induced by the teachers, the range and nature of these could be questioned. This might involve enquiry into the education of infants' teachers, and how, in my observations, its products claimed no special body of knowledge other than that of children and their learning, but were sometimes ignorant of that knowledge which they defined everyone should have (Chapter 5). This implies that the child-centred education of teachers requires supplementing with more general education.

The three R's

In Chapter 4, I reported the primacy that teachers gave to the three R's. It may be thought an absurd question to pose whether children should learn to read, write, and do sums. Most people would regard these as being basic competences for adult life in contemporary British society, although Neil Postman (1973) has questioned the necessity of being able to read, a skill required in order to understand the argument he has written.

The child-centred ideology does not justify the learning of the three R's, but the methods of teaching and learning them were based upon the presumed nature of the child, and his presumed interests. Given the varying definitions of reading readiness by teachers (Chapter 4) and their invariably real consequences, the concept of readiness would appear to be very questionable, indeed at Burnley Road some teachers had laid it aside (Chapter 11). This suggests that some children not manifesting 'readiness' could be started reading earlier in their school careers. This does not automatically mean that they would become better readers.

The content of the reading provided for children is based upon their imputed interests and upon assumptions about the need to protect their innocence (Chapter 3). Does the nature of the story worlds so presented contribute to the sex and social class differences in reading attainment? (The latter was suggested by the Plowden Committee.) The worlds of Peter and Jane, and of Ken, Pat, and Pipkin are clearly more middle class than working class. Would their reading levels rise if the children of Burnley Road read stories reflecting their own family lives, including absent fathers and successions of 'uncles' (Chapter 10)? I do not wish to underestimate the effects that reading can have upon the human consciousness; to do so would be to ignore the manifest consequences of much religious and political writing. But on the specific point a number of reservations must be made. Firstly, children learn to order the realities of the worlds they read about (Chapter 3). Peter and Jane's world was unlike any child's world in that it was a story world, a reality removed from the everyday world. Elliston and Williams (1971) found children of all social classes preferred the Ladybird readers to those of the Nippers Series (Berg, 1968), which were written to appeal to working-class children. Secondly, what would happen at Seaton Park or even Langley? Would children have readers assigned to them according to their class of origin? Thirdly, how would the sex differences in reading attainment relate to this? Many studies, for example Wietzman's (1972), of children's books have shown how girls are typically presented as passive and boys as active. The worlds of Peter and Jane, and of Ken, Pat, and Pipkin are not exceptions to this. But whatever implications this has for the identities of girls it has no obvious disadvantages for their reading abilities.

The family–home background theory

Teachers created and managed classroom situations in which children exhibited behaviour and progress which the teachers sometimes found incompatible with their definitions of what children should be, and they explained the discrepancies by means of the family–home background theory, which preserved the innocence of the children and their own identities as good teachers and left unquestioned their child-centred ideologies and practices (Chapter 7). The posing of the family–home background theory was made easier, if not actually made possible, by their child-centred practices, which presented them with the 'evidence' of the children's homes and families through their writing, drawing, and talking. Taking an interest in the whole child legitimated knowing about his or her life outside the classroom. Thus the child-centredness permitted the family–home background theory and was protected by it.

It is not easy to imagine a case where a teacher would know nothing of a child's background without changing many established practices. If teachers were to abandon the family–home background theory they would have to conclude that any 'problems' were either due to the children's deficiencies or to their own. The acceptance of either would seriously question their ideologies. If they abandoned the concept of the children's innocence, I suspect they would begin to behave like the deviant teachers described in Chapter 8. But these deviants also subscribed to the family–home background theory. To suspend subscription to the 'theory' might lead to an alternative–perhaps a reversion to the 'innate capacity theory' in which 'deficiencies' in children's behaviour and progress had an immutable biological basis; back to Francis Galton if not Plato.

Infant education—a middle-class institution?

The nature of infant education has been explored mainly in terms of the children's behaviour and progress that were defined as problems by the teachers. From this it might be concluded that it is basically a middle-class institution. There are a number of initial reservations that should be made about this view. Firstly, although there were social class differences in mean reading ages and in teachers' assessments of behaviour and attitude to work, it was not the case that all or even most middle-class children did better than all or most working-class children in the same school (Table 8, Chapter 12; Table 12, Chapter 13). Many working-class were assessed as well behaved and hard working, and had high reading quotients. Statistical differences between social groups draw attention away from their similarities. Secondly, the sex differences in these assessments were arguably bigger than the class ones. Do these make infant education a female education or even a middle-class female one, since it is this group who are assessed most highly?

The use of the term 'social class' with reference to children and their parents, here and in other studies, has been based upon a classification by father's occupation. The limited numbers involved have meant that a crude, dichotomous, working-class–middle-class distinction has been used, but it would be more acceptable to refer to middle classes and working classes, sub-divisions at least hinted at in the recognition of children from professional homes at the Langley school (Chapter 12), and in the differences between the working-class children of Burnley Road whose fathers had mainly semi-skilled and unskilled manual occupations, and those of Seaton Park where skilled manual workers predominated (Chapter 9). A man's occupation is the most powerful single clue to his economic and social condition, and so is an index of both class and status in Weberian terms (1948). Thus the common use of social class defined by occupation incorporates these two related aspects.

Studies such as the Newsons's (1976) have shown social class variations in family life and child rearing, both aspects of status culture with clear class connotations in terms of access to such things as housing (see Chapter 12). In the last chapter I suggested that infants' teachers' ideologies were best regarded as a part of their status culture. The question, is infant education a middle-class institution, is therefore better asked in the form of, does the professional status culture of infants' teachers resemble elements of the status culture of the middle classes more than elements of that of the working classes? On the basis of my research and the other studies referred to, I conclude that in terms of teacher–child relationships, models of behaviour and forms of knowledge, infant education has a closer affinity to their equivalents in the families of the middle classes than those of the working classes, a conclusion implied in my support of the family socialization theory in Chapter 14.

If, in crude terms, infant education is more middle class than working class, should it be changed to reverse the emphasis, and what form would it then take? In America the equivalents of the E.P.A. child have been called 'culturally deprived'. This term is sociological nonsense since no one can be deprived of their culture, except perhaps by long periods of isolation from all human contacts. The term is an evaluative one in which the presenting culture of the ghetto children, usually black, is judged to be inferior or deficient. This has been called the 'vacuum ideology', the model of the child that has to be filled up with 'culture'. Critics of this view, such as Nell Keddie (1973), have suggested it is made from a middle-class perspective, and that the culture that the working-class child must be filled up with, although sometimes called 'main-stream culture', is middle-class culture.

Cultural relativity is a sociological view of cultures which makes no evaluation when comparing them, but examines the qualities of each in terms of the part they play in the lives of those who share the culture. This perspective is illustrated by Gladwyn's (1973) comparisons of the navigation methods of Western culture with those of the Trukese. By extension it is argued by the Baratzes (1972) that Negro culture is as 'good' as white, and working-class culture as 'good' as middle-class, and should be recognized in children's education. The cultural discontinuity argument is stood on its head; teachers fail working-class children because the culture of the school is in conflict with that of the children. Like the self-fulfilling prophecy (Chapter 14) this is an attempt to shift the blame for failure away from the child and put it on to the educational system in general and the teachers in particular.

It is not possible to describe working-class (or middle-class) culture with the same kind of precision as that of the Cherokee or the Trukese, so that the nature of an education based upon it is not easily described. Would it incorporate the rough behaviour and untidiness of some of the children at Burnley Road, and the hedonistic materialism of some at Seaton Park? Would 'All things bright and beautiful' be replaced by the pop songs and television jingles of the children's 'presenting culture'? Would the teachers be 'modelled' on working-class mothers who the Newsons (1976) have shown are more likely to smack their children and discipline them according to their own moods than middle-class mothers, and to be less likely to read and give explanations to them? Would the working-class children at Seaton Park and Langley be taught different things in different ways from their middle-class peers? Would the social classes be put into different school classes or even different schools? Should similar considerations be made of the education of boys and girls?

Does cultural relativity answer the question about the nature of an education for working-class infants? Whatever its validity in examining the education of the Cherokee or even the American Negro, a relativist view on this question is not very acceptable. Relativism has a valuable place in sociology, if only to guard against making value-judgements of alien cultures. But value-judgements are the essence of education. The cultural elements of knowledge, beliefs, and behaviour are selected for transmission because they are considered better or more important than others. The sociological equality of cultures is not an argument for such equality in educational practice.

The analysis of the existing system of infant education cannot ignore its relation to the social and economic structure, but this relationship is not a sufficient criterion for its evaluation, which depends principally upon the acceptability of the value-judgements upon which it is based. In the teachers' terms these were that children should be able to read, write, and do sums; they should experience painting, drawing, craft work, singing, dancing, and physical exercise; they should be happy, helpful, quiet, tidy, clean, and kind. They should learn through play and through their presumed interests, and treated in such a way as to protect and respect their imputed innocence. These are posed as intrinsically valuable for all young children irrespective of their sex, social origins, or social destinies. From this point of view infant education may be regarded as the most egalitarian sector of English education.

In conclusion

In the introduction, I described the dilemma of sociologists of education in writing for a dual readership. Most books about infant education are pre-scriptive, saying what ought to happen rather than what may be seen to happen, and they leave almost totally unexamined the ideological basis of the pedagogy and curriculum they endorse. I hope that the descriptions and analyses I have made will be useful and illuminating to student teachers in introducing them to the unfamiliar, and to headteachers and teachers in presenting the familiar in an unfamiliar way, and in helping them, and others, in answering the figurative question about the nature of infant education posed in the title of the book.

I hope also to have made a contribution to the sociological studies of education and something to the dialogue about the nature of the sociology of education. The book illustrates my opinion that sociologists of the education should be empirical rather than speculative, more analytical than critical, and should examine value-judgements rather than make them. Our theories should not be abstractions, but should be related to the activities we attempt to explain in a way that respects the complexity of the educational process and its basic humanity.

For the sake of both kinds of reader I have tried not to lose sight of the teachers and children whose relationships are at the heart of infant education.

Bibliography

Ariès, P. (1962), *Centuries of Childhood*, Cape.

Baratz, S., and Baratz, J. E. (1972), 'Negro ghetto children and urban education: a culture solution', *Social Education*, **33**.

Bechhofer, F. (1974), 'Current approaches to empirical research: some central ideas', in *Approaches to Sociology*, J. Rex (Ed.), Routledge & Kegan Paul.

Bennett, S. N., and Jordan, J. (1975), 'A typology of teaching styles in primary schools', *British Journal of Educational Psychology*, **45**.

Bereiter, C., and Engelmann, S. (1966), *Teaching Disadvantaged Children in the PreSchool*, Prentice-Hall.

Berg, L. (1968), Nippers Series, Macmillan.

Bernstein, B. (1975) 'Class and pedagogies. Visible and invisible', in *Class Codes and Control*, vol. 3., Routledge & Kegan Paul.

Bernstein, B., *et al.* (1966), 'Ritual in education', *Philosophical Transactions of the Royal Society of London*, B, 251.

Bernstein, B., and Davies, B. (1969), 'Some sociological comments on Plowden', in *Perspectives on Plowden*, ed. R. S. Peters, Routledge & Kegan Paul.

Bourdieu, P., and Passeron, J. C. (1977), *Reproduction in Education Society and Culture*, Sage.

Boyce, E. R. (1950), Gay Way Series, Macmillan.

Brandis, W., and Bernsetein, B. (1974), *Selection and Control*, Routledge & Kegan Paul.

Central Advisory Committee (1967), *Children and their Primary Schools* (Plowden Report), H.M.S.O.

Cicourel, A. B. (1964), *Method and Measurement in Sociology*, Free Press.

Clark, B. R. (1962), *Educating the Expert Society*, Chandler.

Collins, R. (1977), 'Some comparative principles of educational stratification', *Harvard Educational Review*, **47**.

De Vries, L. (ed.) (1965), *Flowers of Delight*, Dobson.

Elliston, T., and Williams, W. (1971), 'Social class and children's reading preferences', *Readings*, **1**.

Esland, G. M. (1971), 'Teaching and learning as the organisation of knowledge', in *Knowledge and Control*, ed. M. F. D. Young, Macmillan.

Fagg, R. (1962), *Everyday Writing*, U.L.P.

Flanders, N. A. (1970), *Analysing Teaching Behaviour*, Addison-Wesley.

Fletcher, H., *et al.* (1970), *Mathematics for Schools*, Addison-Wesley.

Fuchs, E. (1973), 'How teachers learn to help children fail', in Keddie (1973).

Garfinkel, H. (1967), *Studies in Ethnomethodology*, Prentice-Hall.

Gladwyn, T. L. (1973), 'Culture and logical process', in Keddie (1973).

Glaser, B. G., and Strauss, A. L. (1968), *The Discovery of Grounded Theory*, Weidenfeld & Nicolson.

Goffman, E. (1961), *Encounters*, Bobbs-Merrill.

Gorbutt, D. (1972), 'The new sociology of education', *Education for Teaching*, **89**.

Hargreaves, D. H. (1967), *Social Relations in a Secondary School*, Routledge & Kegan Paul.

Hartley, J. D. (1977), 'Some consequences of teachers' definitions of boys and girls in two infants' schools', unpublished Ph.D. thesis, University of Exeter.

Hume, E. and Wheeler, E. C. (1972), *My First Book of Sums*, Evans.

Jones, J., and Bernstein, B. (1974), 'The preparation of the infant-school child', Appendix to Brandis and Bernstein (1974).

Keddie, N. (1971), 'Classroom knowledge', in *Knowledge and Control*, M. F. D. Young (Ed.), Macmillan.

Keddie, N. (1973), Editor's Introduction to *Tinker, Tailor. The Myth of Cultural Deprivation*, Penguin.

King, R. A. (1971), 'Unequal access in education—sex and social class', *Social and Economic Administration*, **5**.

King, R. A. (1973), *School Organisation and Pupil Involvement*, Routledge & Kegan Paul.

King, R. A. (1976a), *School and College—Studies of Post-Sixteen Education*, Routledge & Kegan Paul.

King, R. A. (1976b), 'Bernstein's sociology of the school—some propositions tested', *British Journal of Sociology*, **27**

King, R. A. (1977), *Education*, Social Structure of Modern Britain Series, 2nd edition, Longman.

Kounin, J. S. (1970), *Discipline and Group Management in Classrooms*, Holt, Rinehart, & Winston.

Little, A. N., *et al.* (1971), 'Do small classes help?', *New Society*, **18**.

Madsen, C. H., *et al.* (1968), 'Rules, praise and ignoring', *Journal of Applied Behavioural Analysis*, **1**.

Mathews, M. M. (1966), *Teaching to Read—Historically Considered*, University of Chicago Press.

Mennell, S. J. (1974), *Sociological Theory: Uses and Unities*, Nelson.

Merton, R. K. (1959), Introduction to *Sociology Today*, ed. R. K. Merton *et al.* Basic Books.

Merton, R. K. (1968), *Social Theory and Social Structure*, Routledge & Kegan Paul.

Mills, C. W. (1959), *The Sociological Imagination*, Penguin.

Moran, P. R. (1971), 'The integrated day', *Educational Research*, **14**.

Murry, W. (1969), Key Words Reading Scheme, Ladybird.

Newson, J., and Newson, E. (1976), *Seven Year Olds in the Home Environment*, Allen & Unwin.

Opie, I., and Opie, P. (1958), *The Lore and Language of Children*, Oxford University Press.

Parsons, T. (1961), 'The school class as a social system: some of its functions in American society', in *Education, Economy and Society*, ed. A. H. Halsey *et al.*, Free Press.

Pinchbeck, I., and Hewitt, M. (1973), *Children in English Society*, vol. II, Routledge & Kegan Paul.

Postman, N. (1973), 'The politics of reading', in Keddie (1973).

Rex, J. (1973), *Discovering Sociology*, Routledge & Kegan Paul.

Rist, R. (1970), 'Student social class and teacher expectations: the self-fulfilling prophecy in ghetto education', *Harvard Educational Review*, **40**.

Rosenthal, R., and Jacobson, L. (1968), *Pygmalion in the Classroom*, Holt.

Schutz, A. (1967), *Collected Papers Vol. 1 The Problem of Social Reality*, Nijhoft.

Schutz, A. (1932, 1972), *The Phenomenology of the Social World*, Heinemann.

Schutz, A. (1953), 'Concept and theory formation in the social sciences', *Journal of Philosophy*, **51**.

Sendak, M. (1967), *Where the Wild Things Are*, Bodley Head.

Sharp, R., and Green, A. (1975), *Education and Social Control*, Routledge & Kegan Paul.

Silberman, C. E. (1970), *Crisis in the Classroom*, Wildwood House.

Thomas, W. I. (1928), *The Child in America*, Knopf.

Weber, M. (1904, 1930), *The Protestant Ethic and the Spirit of Capitalism*, Allen & Unwin.

Weber, M. (1922, 1968), *Economy and Society*, Bedminster.

Weber, M. (1948), *Essays in Sociology*, Routledge & Kegan Paul.

Weber, M. (1964), *The Theory of Social and Economic Organisation*, Free Press.

Weinberg, M. S. (1965), 'Sexual modesty, social meanings and the nudist camp, *Social Problems*, **12**.

Weitzman, L. J., *et al.* (1972), 'Sex role specialisation in picture books for preschool children', *American Journal of Sociology*, **77**.

Whitbread, N. (1972), *The Evolution of the Nursery-Infant School*, Routledge & Kegan Paul.

Whitty, G. (1974), 'Sociology and the problem of radical educational change', in *Educability, Schools and Ideology*, M. Flude and J. Ahier (Eds.), Croom Helen.

Whyte, W. F. (1955), *Corner Boys*, 2nd edition, University of Chicago Press.

Woodhead, M. (1976), *Intervening in Disadvantage*, N.F.E.R.

Young, D. (1968), *Manual to the Group Reading Test*, U.L.P.

Zolotow, C. (1968), *Mr. Rabbit and the Lovely Present*, Bodley Head.

Index

154